Colleges of Cambridge

A complete guide to the
31 Colleges of Cambridge University

Photography © Andrew Pearce ARPS
Design & editing: Debi Pearce

First published 2015 © Fotogenix Publishing
Printed in England by Swallowtail Print Ltd

www.fotogenix.co.uk
ISBN 978-0-9547355-4-8

Also by Fotogenix Publishing: 'Cambridge: A Photographic Portrait'
'The Cambridge Companion' • 'Welcome to Cambridge' • 'A BIG Welcome to Cambridge'

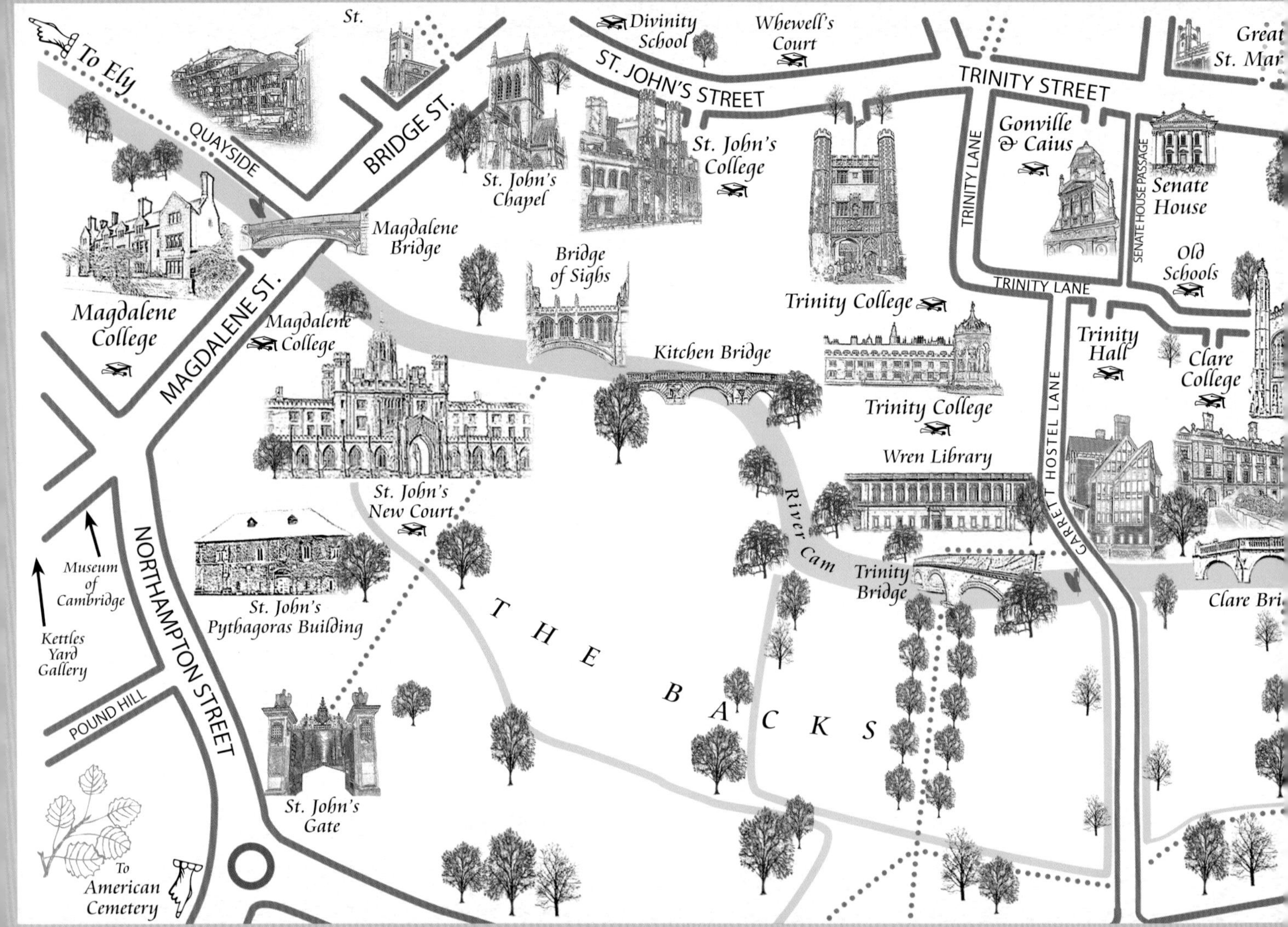

To Ely
St.
Divinity School
Whewell's Court
Great St. Mar
QUAYSIDE
BRIDGE ST.
ST. JOHN'S STREET
TRINITY STREET
St. John's Chapel
St. John's College
Gonville & Caius
TRINITY LANE
SENATE HOUSE PASSAGE
Senate House
Magdalene Bridge
Bridge of Sighs
Old Schools
TRINITY LANE
Trinity College
Magdalene College
MAGDALENE ST.
Magdalene College
Kitchen Bridge
Trinity Hall
Clare College
Trinity College
GARRETT HOSTEL LANE
Wren Library
St. John's New Court
River Cam
Museum of Cambridge
NORTHAMPTON STREET
Trinity Bridge
Clare Bri
St. John's Pythagoras Building
Kettles Yard Gallery
THE BACKS
POUND HILL
St. John's Gate
To American Cemetery

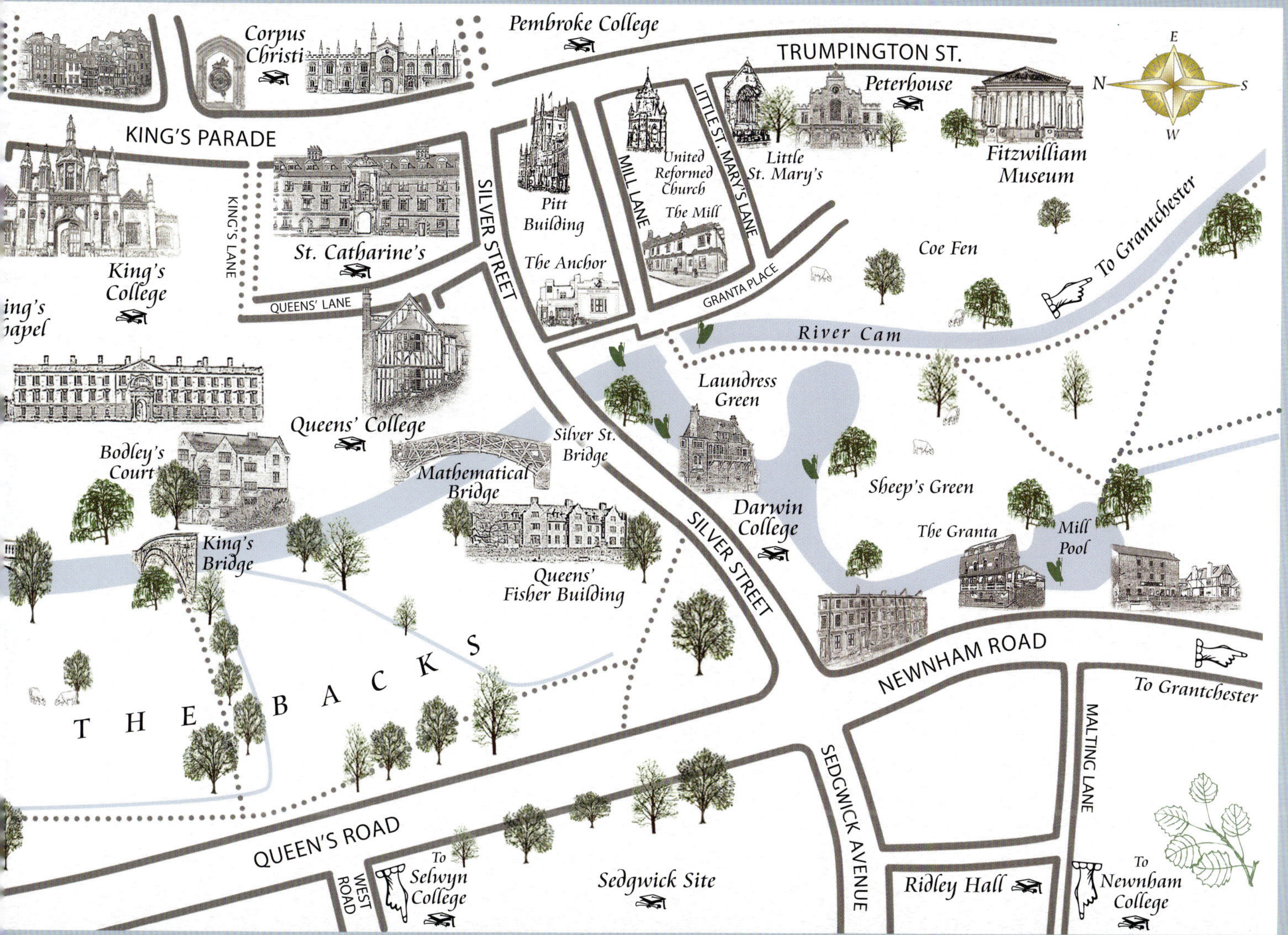

Corpus Christi
Pembroke College
TRUMPINGTON ST.
Peterhouse
E
N
S
W
Fitzwilliam Museum
KING'S PARADE
KING'S LANE
St. Catharine's
King's College
ing's
hapel
QUEENS' LANE
SILVER STREET
Pitt Building
The Anchor
MILL LANE
United Reformed Church
The Mill
LITTLE ST. MARY'S LANE
Little St. Mary's
GRANTA PLACE
Coe Fen
To Grantchester
River Cam
Laundress Green
Queens' College
Bodley's Court
Silver St. Bridge
Mathematical Bridge
Darwin College
Sheep's Green
The Granta
Mill Pool
King's Bridge
Queens' Fisher Building
SILVER STREET
NEWNHAM ROAD
To Grantchester
THE BACKS
MALTING LANE
SEDGWICK AVENUE
QUEEN'S ROAD
WEST ROAD
To Selwyn College
Sedgwick Site
Ridley Hall
To Newnham College

CAMBRIDGE TOWN

Cambridge may be famous for its University but, before the first scholars arrived in 1209, invading forces all favoured its strategic importance. Why? Cambridgeshire is a flat, marshy county. But here at Cambridge there was a hill, conveniently beside a shallow crossing place on the river. As an added bonus, Cambridge could be reached from the coast - great for trade until fenland drainage caused the river to silt up in the 1600s. Even then, the river remained a valuable trade route until the railway opened in 1845. In 1215 the town was enclosed for protection with a ditch, named the King's Ditch. This may have been effective against human foes, but it left Cambridge vulnerable to other enemies! This filthy ditch bred rats, and their fleas brought dreadful plague - the Black Death. For centuries Cambridge suffered, but relief came in 1610, when Town and Gown collaborated to create Hobson's Conduit - a fresh water supply system which was significantly sponsored by carrier Thomas Hobson, who ran a stable in town.

400	The Romans departed
800	1st record of river crossing at site of Magdalene Bridge
1025	St. Bene't's Church built
1068	Normans built castle on Castle Mound
1130	Round Church built - one of only 4 in the country
1209	University founded
1215	Town enclosed, and King's Ditch dug
1521	John Siberch began printing at Cambridge
1539	King Henry VIII suppressed the monasteries
1553	Queen Mary Tudor began reprisals against Protestants
1614	Hobson's Conduit finished
1616	Oliver Cromwell attended Sidney Sussex College
1638	Clare Bridge built by Thomas Grumbold
1642	English Civil War - Cromwell destroyed many Catholic college treasures
1660	King Charles II restored to the throne
1749	Queens' Mathematical Bridge built
1766	Addenbrooke's founded

4

Cambridge has often found itself centre stage in religious and political dramas, especially Henry VIII's dissolution of the monasteries, and the backlash of his daughter Mary Tudor's religious reprisals. Oliver Cromwell found many Royalist adversaries here during the Civil War. The colleges lost many treasures from their chapels when he sent his henchmen to destroy their Catholic 'superstitious' symbolism. Intermingled with these power struggles were riots of the townspeople, enraged by inequalities between the privileged colleges & their own hardships. The old division between University & townsfolk persists. But this 'Town & Gown' relationship is symbiotic. Income from rents helps the University to maintain its buildings, while local trade depends on tourists. Few cities can equal the culture of Cambridge. Posters everywhere advertise music and drama. Cambridge is proud of its past & nurtures its treasures. Its population is only 125,000, but every year 3,000,000 visitors appreciate its beauty, history and culture.

CAMBRIDGE TOWN

- 1788 — street lighting & paving installed in Cambridge along Petty Cury
- 1845 — Eastern Counties Railway began services to Cambridge station
- 1849 — 'Great Fire' of Cambridge destroyed market square
- 1876 — W. Heffer bookseller began trading
- 1880 — Cambridge Street tramways began operating
- 1897 — Massive celebrations of Queen Victoria's Diamond Jubilee held on Parker's Piece
- 1928 — 1st live radio broadcast of the Festival of 9 Lessons & Carols from King's College
- 1938 — Cambridge Airport opened
- 1951 — Cambridge granted city status
- 1965 — First Cambridge Folk Festival held
- 1973 — Lion Yard shopping centre opened
- 1975 — University founded the Cambridge Science Park
- 1984 — Grafton Centre opened
- 1990 — Royal Greenwich Observatory relocated from London to Cambridge
- 2008 — Grand Arcade fully opened
- 2011 — Prince William became Duke of Cambridge

THE UNIVERSITY

Cambridge University began in 1209, when scholars fleeing from riots in Oxford took refuge here. The first college to be founded was Peterhouse, in 1284. Many early colleges were founded by the Church, others by monarchs wishing to create permanent places of learning, and six of the medieval colleges were created by women! Many colleges were prompted by the ravages of the Black Death in medieval times, when Cambridge urgently needed to replace the great numbers of clergy and learned men who had been lost. Teaching was the domain of the monasteries, although secular teaching developed from around 1284 onwards. Scholars began around age 14, and would have to learn Latin before studying the *Trivium*, in Grammar, Logic & Rhetoric. Then came the *Quadrivium* of Arithmetic, Geometry, Music & Astronomy, qualifying the student to become a lecturer himself as a Master of Arts.

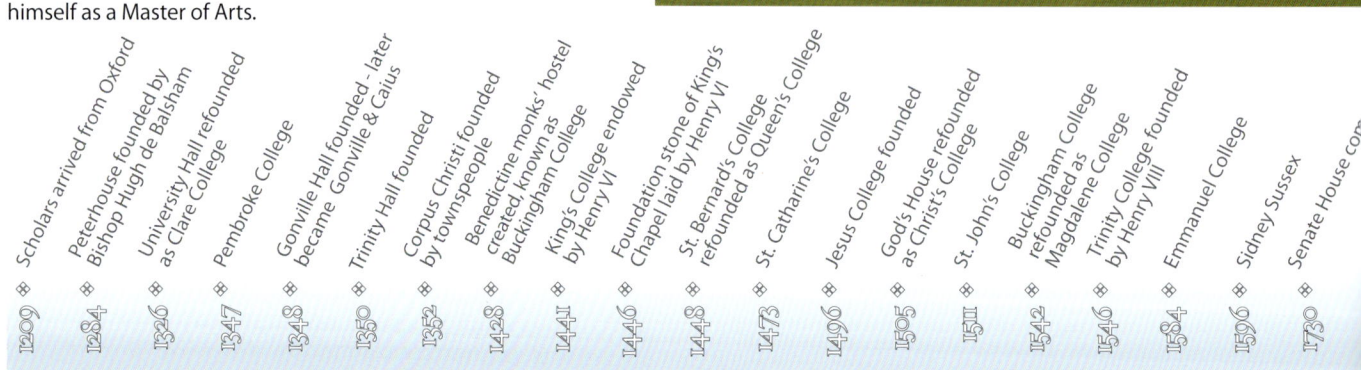

1209	Scholars arrived from Oxford
1284	Peterhouse founded by Bishop Hugh de Balsham
1326	University Hall refounded as Clare College
1347	Pembroke College
1348	Gonville Hall founded - later became Gonville & Caius
1350	Trinity Hall founded
1352	Corpus Christi founded by townspeople
1428	Benedictine monks' hostel created known as Buckingham College
1441	King's College endowed by Henry VI
1446	Foundation stone of King's Chapel laid by Henry VI
1448	St. Bernard's College refounded as Queen's College
1473	St. Catharine's College
1496	Jesus College founded
1505	God's House refounded as Christ's College
1511	St. John's College
1542	Buckingham College refounded as Magdalene College
1546	Trinity College founded by Henry VIII
1584	Emmanuel College
1596	Sidney Sussex
1730	Senate House com...

Old Schools & Senate House

Sidney Sussex was the last 'medieval' college to be founded. 200 years passed before the University began to expand again when Downing College was created in 1800. Women were given their own colleges (Newnham and Girton) in the late 1800s. But it was not until 1948 that women were first admitted to full degrees, and 25 years longer before the other colleges began to accept women. Degree ceremonies take place throughout the year in Senate House, with the majority happening in June. Immaculate ranks of *graduands* process through the streets from their respective colleges, emerging from the ceremony into Senate House Passage as fully-fledged *graduates*. Today there are 31 Colleges, and around 15,000 students. The most recent college is Robinson, founded in 1979, but a major new University community is under construction near Madingley Road - might there soon be 32 colleges?

THE UNIVERSITY

- Botanic Garden founded near Corpus Christi College
- 1800 ❋ Downing College - the 1st college for 200 years
- 1816 ❋ Fitzwilliam Museum founded
- 1829 ❋ 1st Oxford vs Cambridge Boat Race
- 1846 ❋ Botanic Garden relocated to Trumpington Road
- 1869 ❋ Girton College: the 1st women's college
- 1871 ❋ Newnham College, the 2nd college for women
- 1882 ❋ Selwyn College
- 1885 ❋ Hughes Hall founded as the Cambridge Training College for Women
- 1896 ❋ St. Edmund's College
- 1934 ❋ University Library founded by Sir Giles Gilbert Scott
- 1954 ❋ New Hall: the 3rd women's college
- 1960 ❋ Churchill College
- 1964 ❋ Darwin College
- 1965 ❋ Clare Hall, Lucy Cavendish & Wolfson College
- 1966 ❋ Fitzwilliam College formally constituted
- 1972 ❋ Churchill College became the 1st to admit women
- 1976 ❋ Homerton College formally adopted into the University
- 1979 ❋ Robinson College: the latest, and 31st college
- 1988 ❋ Magdalene became the last college to admit women
- 2008 ❋ New Hall became Murray Edwards College
- 2009 ❋ 800th Anniversary of Cambridge University

PETERHOUSE

Peterhouse is Cambridge's oldest college, founded in 1284 by Bishop Hugh de Balsham in emulation of 'the Oxford Scholars of Merton, studiously engaged in the pursuit of literature'. During the political turbulence of the 1600s, Master Andrew Perne survived by simply adopting the view of the moment, ensuring both the college's and his own job's security! Perne instigated Hobson's Conduit, which brought clean water to Cambridge. The chapel was built by Matthew Wren, uncle of Sir Christopher Wren. The garden is beautiful in spring, and has an ancient wall with a bricked-up door displaying the crests of 2 bishops of Ely. A branch of the Cam once led to this door, and bishops could visit from Ely by boat. Many scientific innovators studied here, including Cockerell, Whittle, Babbage, and Cavendish. In 1884 Lord Kelvin marked the college's 600th anniversary by making Peterhouse the 2nd place in England to receive electric lighting.

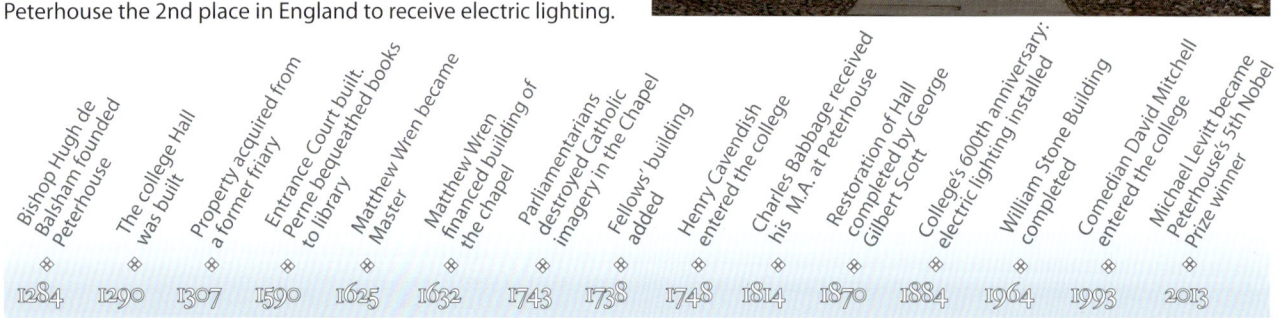

1284	Bishop Hugh de Balsham founded Peterhouse
1290	The college Hall was built
1307	Property acquired from a former friary
1590	Entrance Court built; Perne bequeathed books to library
1625	Matthew Wren became Master
1632	Matthew Wren financed building of the chapel
1643	Parliamentarians destroyed Catholic imagery in the Chapel
1738	Fellows' building added
1748	Henry Cavendish entered the college
1814	Charles Babbage received his M.A. at Peterhouse
1870	Restoration of Hall completed by George Gilbert Scott
1884	College's 600th anniversary: electric lighting installed
1964	William Stone Building completed
1993	Comedian David Mitchell entered the college
2013	Michael Levitt became Peterhouse's 5th Nobel Prize winner

Clare College began in 1326 as *University Hall*, but was refounded in 1338, when Lady Elizabeth de Clare came to its financial rescue. She was 3 times widowed: the golden tears round the black-bordered college arms represent her bereavement. During the early years the college lacked resources and in 1548 it narrowly escaped amalgamation with nearby Trinity Hall, thanks to intervention by religious reformer Nicholas Ridley. It also suffered two fires, which destroyed many of its early records. Clare possesses Cambridge's oldest stone bridge, built in 1638 by Thomas Grumbold for a payment of just 3 shillings! Old Court, "more like a palace than a college", evolved over 77 years, largely influenced by architect James Essex. The chapel, which was consecrated in 1769, is exceptionally pretty, with its ethereally lit lantern tower and beautiful stained glass. Clare was one of the first three colleges to admit female students. Famous members include naturalist Sir David Attenborough and composer John Rutter.

CLARE

1326	Richard de Badew founded University Hall
1338	Lady Elizabeth de Clare re-founded college as Clare Hall
1362	Fire destroyed the college's Hall
1510	Religious Reformer Hugh Latimer elected as a Fellow of the college
1521	Fire destroyed Master's chambers, treasury and archives
1638	Rebuilding began with Thomas Grumbold's stone bridge
1642	Civil War interrupted building work
1662	Building recommenced: Old Court begun
1715	Construction of Master's Lodge completed the rebuilding of Old Court
1763	Burrough and Essex built chapel
1856	Clare Hall renamed Clare College
1926	Memorial Court built, commemorating 200 members lost in WW1
1947	Nevill Willmer re-designed Fellows' Garden
1972	Clare became one of the 1st three colleges to admit female students
1975	Composer John Rutter became Director of Music
2005	James Watson unveiled commemorative DNA sculpture

9

PEMBROKE

The third oldest college was founded in 1347 by Marie, Countess of Pembroke, who may have been inspired by her friend Elizabeth de Clare. Pembroke has always been highly respected: Queen Elizabeth I proclaimed it *"O domus antiqua et religiosa!"* (O ancient & devout house!) Matthew Wren studied at Pembroke but became Master of Peterhouse. He was imprisoned by Cromwell for 18 years, and resolved to build a chapel for Pembroke should he ever be free again. This became his nephew Christopher Wren's 1st ever commission. Britain's youngest Prime Minister, William Pitt, entered the college aged only 14. In the 1750s, poet Thomas Gray joined the college in preference to nearby Peterhouse; poets Edmund Spenser and Ted Hughes also studied here. Pembroke lost one fifth of its serving members in WW1- more than any other college. Happier times more recently have nurtured the careers of Bill Oddie & Tim Brooke-Taylor.

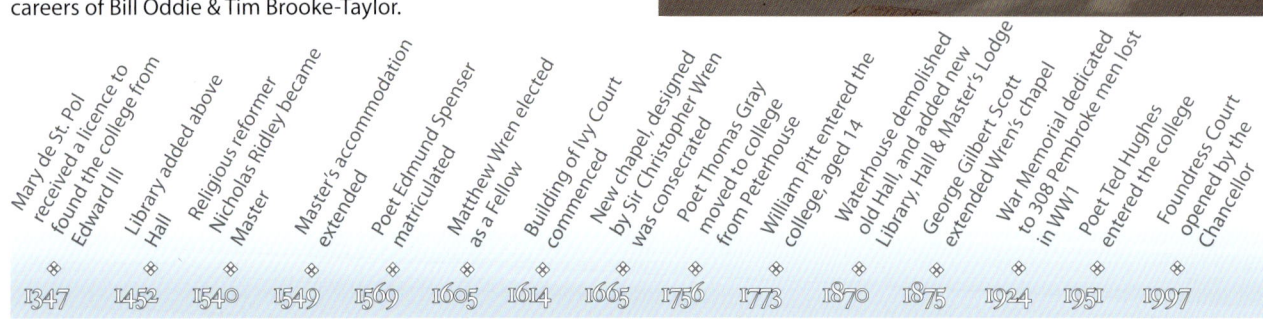

1347	Mary de St. Pol received a licence to found the college from Edward III
1452	Library added above Hall
1540	Religious reformer Nicholas Ridley became Master
1549	Master's accommodation extended
1569	Poet Edmund Spenser matriculated
1605	Matthew Wren elected as a Fellow
1614	Building of Ivy Court commenced
1665	New chapel, designed by Sir Christopher Wren was consecrated
1756	Poet Thomas Gray moved to college from Peterhouse
1773	William Pitt entered the college, aged 14
1870	Waterhouse demolished old Hall, and added new Library, Hall & Master's Lodge
1875	George Gilbert Scott extended Wren's chapel
1924	War Memorial dedicated to 308 Pembroke men lost in WW1
1951	Poet Ted Hughes entered the college
1997	Foundress Court opened by the Chancellor

GONVILLE & CAIUS

Norfolk rector Edmund Gonville commenced this college's foundation during a terrible visitation of the plague in 1348. When he himself died 3 years later, his friend Bishop Bateman, provided funding & relocated it next door to his own college, Trinity Hall. After years of poverty its fortunes changed when it was refounded by the rich doctor, John Keys, who changed his name to a Latinised form, *Caius*, after travelling in Italy. He became Master in 1559. Caius loved decorative symbolism. To inspire his scholars, he installed 3 gates. Students enter modestly via the Gate of Humility, pass daily through the Gate of Virtue, & depart on Graduation Day from the Gate of Honour. The chapel displays an impressive memorial to Caius, (complete with a cast of his skull!). The college is famous for science & medicine: with 13 Nobel Prize winners. Members include William Harvey, who discovered the circulation of blood, and James Chadwick, discoverer of the neutron.

1348	Edmund Gonville founded Gonville Hall
1351	William Bateman, Bishop of Norwich, took over development of college
1529	John Keys, later Caius, entered college as a student
1557	Dr Caius refounded college as Gonville & Caius
1573	Caius resigned and died following destruction of his Catholic treasures by Puritan college officials
1751	William Burrough updated Gonville Court
1868	Waterhouse replaced Tree Court buildings, and built tower
1912	Dr Wilson took college flag on Scott's ill-fated Antarctic expedition
1919	Athlete Harold Abrahams, depicted in *Chariots of Fire* entered the college
1921	1st & only Oxford/Cambridge air race, won by Caius' W. Philcox
1960	Development of Harvey Court on West Road
1979	Gonville & Caius admitted women students and Fellows
2013	Michael Levitt became most recent Nobel Laureate (Chemistry)
2013	James Watson unveiled memorial commemorating 60 years since discovery of DNA structure

TRINITY HALL

Trinity Hall's appearance belies its age due to renovations in the 1700s. It was founded in 1350 to train lawyers lost to the plague. These lawyers were often required to travel to London, and in 1725 Trinity Hall instigated milestones to assist their journey, starting from Great St. Mary's church. The tune for Great St. Mary's chimes, composed by Trinity Hall's Dr Jowett, is better known as the sound of *Big Ben* in London. The chapel is the smallest in either Cambridge or Oxford, with a ceiling displaying benefactors' coats of arms, a superb painting of the Holy Family behind the altar, and candlesticks bearing the distinctive crescent emblem of the college. The Elizabethan library, with some books on chains, houses amongst its treasures a work by Erasmus, the Dutch philosopher, published in 1521. Trinity Hall's new Jerwood Library is the most recent building along the Cam. The college has a beautiful garden by the river, which was famous for its massive chestnut trees until these succumbed to disease.

1350	William Bateman founded the college
1366	Chapel built: the smallest in Cambridge or Oxford
1730	College provided milestones along route to London
1761	Museum founder Viscount Fitzwilliam attended the college
1776	Alumnus Arthur Middleton signed US Declaration of Independence
1794	Composition of Westminster chimes for Great St. Mary's
1850	Fire destroyed east side of First Court
1852	Salvin rebuilt First Court
1898	Electric lighting was installed
1935	Addition of North Court
1952	United Nations leader Hans Blix entered the college
1956	Robert Runcie became college Dean
1962	Theoretical physicist, Stephen Hawking, studied at the college
1977	The college admitted female students
1988	Jerwood Library built

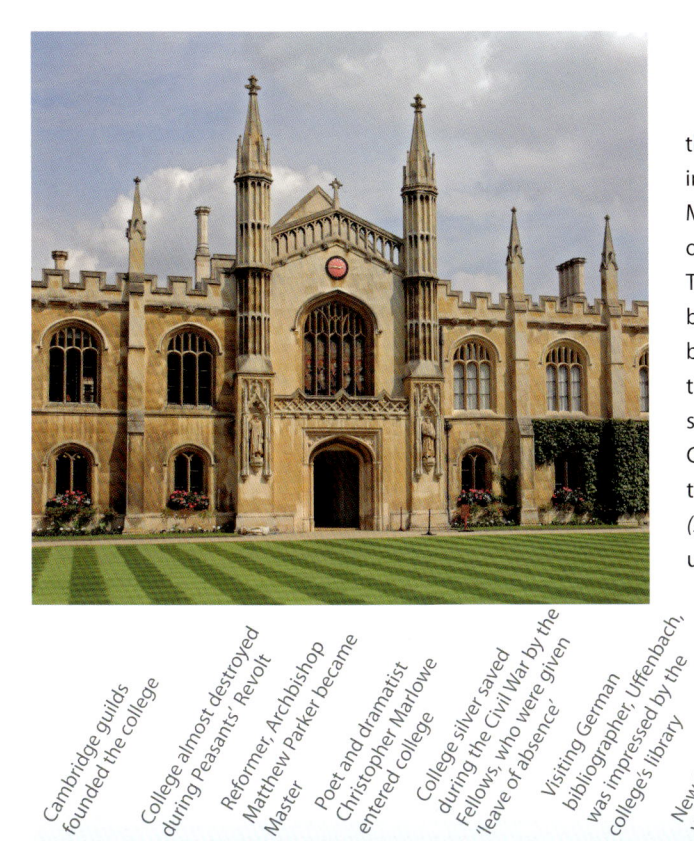

Corpus Christi was born out of necessity in 1352, when Cambridge needed to replace the priests who had been lost to the plague. Unusually, this college was founded by the townspeople themselves - an initiative by the guilds of Corpus Christi and the Blessed Virgin Mary. However, this did not protect it from attack and ransacking of its books and treasures during the Peasants' Revolt of 1381. The college today has a magnificent collection of precious books, many of which were amassed by Matthew Parker, who became Master in 1544. When plague struck again in the 1630s, the Master Henry Butts remained, after all had fled, to tend the sick, but the horror drove him to suicide. Corpus Christi has Cambridge University's oldest medieval court, and also one of the most modern features of all the colleges, the Corpus Clock *(see P48)*. Conceived and funded by Dr John C. Taylor, it was unveiled by physicist Stephen Hawking in 2008.

1352	Cambridge guilds founded the college
1381	College almost destroyed during Peasants' Revolt
1544	Reformer Archbishop Matthew Parker became Master
1581	Poet and dramatist Christopher Marlowe entered college
1643	College silver saved during the Civil War by the Fellows, who were given 'leave of absence'
1710	Visiting German bibliographer, Uffenbach, was impressed by the college's library
1827	New Court designed by William Wilkins
1904	Sighting of a ghost, which 3 undergraduates attempted to exorcise
1919	Old Court restored by T.H. Lyon
1953	A painting dated 1585 discovered during renovation, but now proved not to be of Christopher Marlowe
1962	Leckhampton site developed for research students
2008	Corpus Clock unveiled by Stephen Hawking

CORPUS CHRISTI

MAGDALENE

Magdalene's original red brick buildings were first used in 1428 as a hostel for monks. In 1542, following Henry VIII's dissolution of the monasteries, his Lord Chancellor Thomas Audley renamed it 'The College of St. Mary Magdalene'. Audley, whose descendants today retain the right to appoint the college's Master, ordered that *Magdalene* should be spelled *Maudleyn* to include his own name! Samuel Pepys, renowned writer and *bon viveur*, studied here in 1650. His library was given to the college in 1724. Pepys may have enjoyed a drink or two, but in the later 1700s the college abstained from alcohol, instead rendering the river 'unnavigable with tea-leaves'. C.S. Lewis, author of the *Narnia* books, studied here, and A.C. Benson, who wrote the words for *Land of Hope & Glory* was Magdalene's Master for 10 years. During the 1920s the college extended across the road, taking over several existing buildings. In 1988, Magdalene College became the last in the University to admit female students.

1428	Abbot of Crowland gave site for a Benedictine hostel
1542	Lord Thomas Audley refounded the college
1564	The 4th Duke of Norfolk promised funding for completion of the Quadrant
1582	Thomas Nevile, later of Trinity, became Master
1627	Henry Dunster, 1st Principal of Harvard, completed his degree
1651	Samuel Pepys entered the college
1677	The building now known as the Pepys Library was begun
1724	Magdalene received Pepys' collection of 3,000 books
1909	New building in Second Court designed by Sir Aston Webb
1924	Alumnus George Mallory perished in attempt to climb Everest
1932	Lutyens Building completed
1954	First Court's monastic brickwork uncovered
1988	College became the last to admit female students
2001	Nelson Mandela made Honorary Fellow

King Henry VI, aged only 19, founded this college in 1441, and the 90-year process of building his chapel was begun in 1446. It fulfils Henry VI's instructions that the chapel should be "In large fourme clene and substancial, settyng a parte superfluite of too gret curious werkes of entaille and besy moldyng". However, in his original plans the chapel spires would have crowned a forest of turrets. The massive Fellows' Building beside the chapel was begun in 1724. Its foundation stone was originally left abandoned, cut half-way through during the construction of the chapel, when the workmen heard of Henry VI's capture. King's screen and Great Gate were designed by William Wilkins in 1822. Henry VI also founded Eton school, and until 1873 King's College exclusively accepted Eton students, who were automatically granted a degree without examination. Notable alumni include Robert Walpole, Britain's 1st Prime Minister, poet Rupert Brooke, and WW2 Enigma code-breaker Alan Turing.

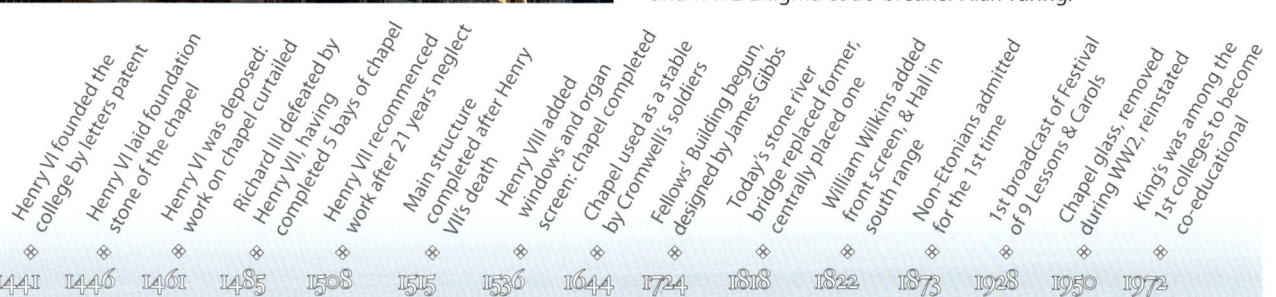

K I N G ' S

- 1441 — Henry VI founded the college by letters patent
- 1446 — Henry VI laid foundation stone of the chapel
- 1461 — Henry VI was deposed; work on chapel curtailed
- 1485 — Richard III defeated by Henry VII, having completed 5 bays of chapel
- 1508 — Henry VII recommenced work after 21 years neglect
- 1515 — Main structure completed after Henry VII's death
- 1536 — Henry VIII added windows and organ screen; chapel completed
- 1644 — Chapel used as a stable by Cromwell's soldiers
- 1724 — Fellows' Building begun, designed by James Gibbs
- 1818 — Today's stone river bridge replaced former, centrally placed one
- 1822 — William Wilkins added front screen, & Hall in south range
- 1873 — Non-Etonians admitted for the 1st time
- 1928 — 1st broadcast of Festival of 9 Lessons & Carols
- 1950 — Chapel glass, removed during WW2, reinstated
- 1972 — King's was among the 1st colleges to become co-educational

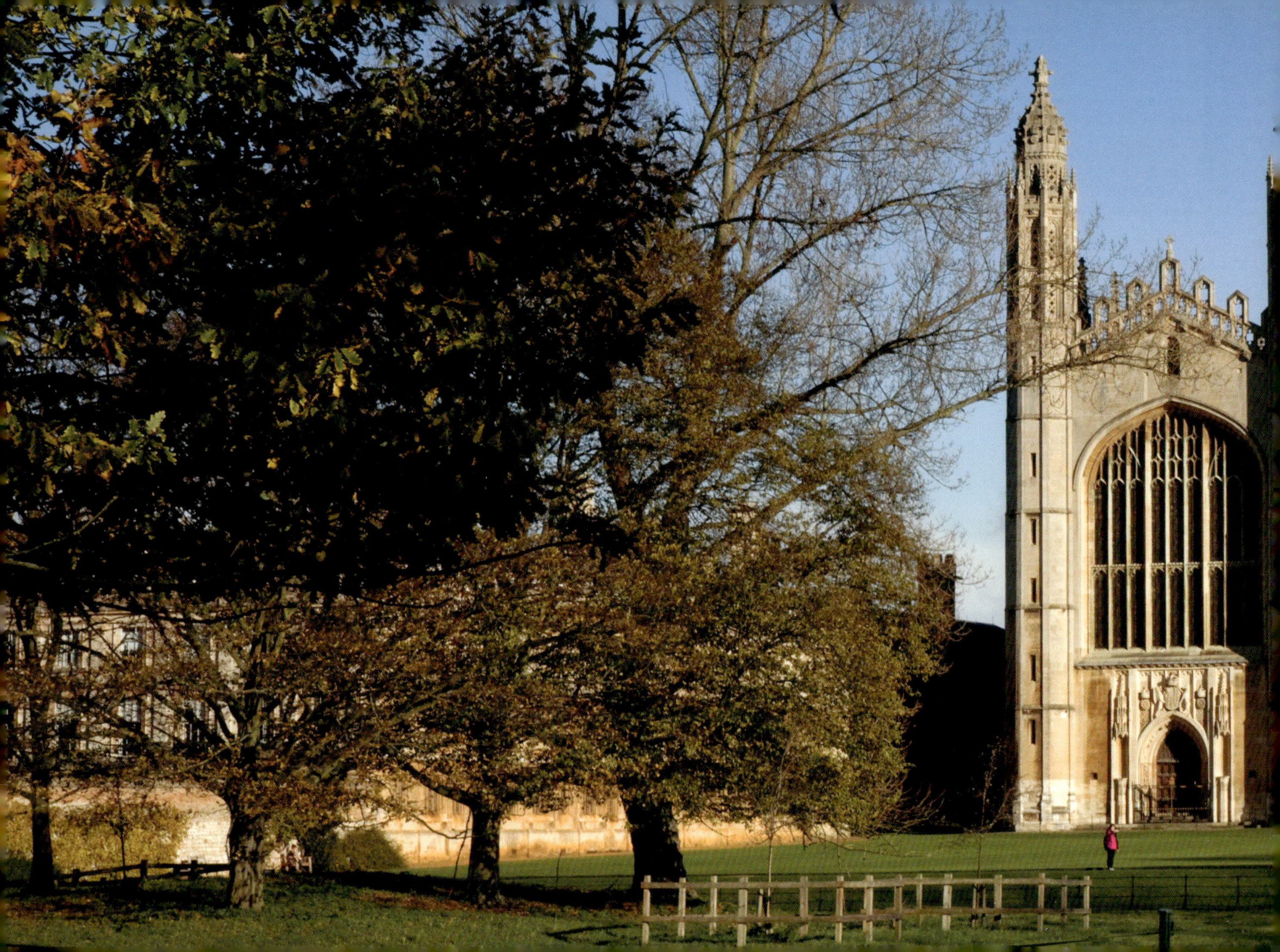

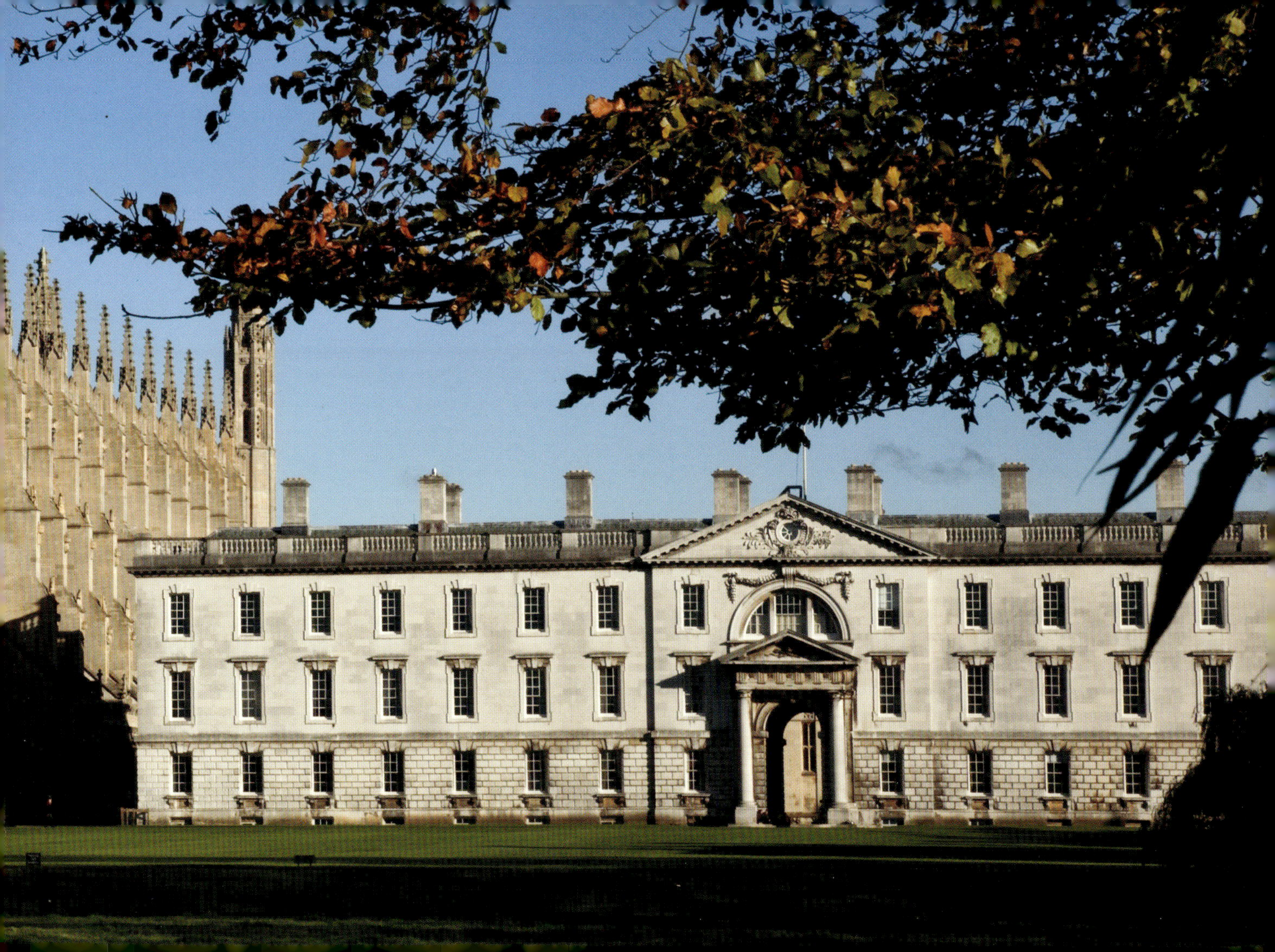

QUEENS'

This college has been associated with several queens! It began as St. Bernard's College, but was refounded in 1446 by Queen Margaret of Anjou, in the year that her husband, Henry VI, laid the foundation stone of the chapel at his own college just along the river. It was developed by her friend Elizabeth Woodville, when she became queen herself as wife of Edward IV. The late Queen Mother was patroness, & has been succeeded by Her Majesty Queen Elizabeth II. Queens' red brick buildings, dating from 1448, are unusual in a town dominated by stonework. They create a sense of warmth & intimacy. Special features include the beautiful cloisters built in 1495, the intricately painted chapel ceiling, and beamed buildings which were plastered over for many years until restoration in 1923. There is also a very unusual combined sundial and moondial. The tower in the corner of Cloister Court was the residence of Dutch philosopher Erasmus in 1510, when he was invited to the college by its Master, John Fisher.

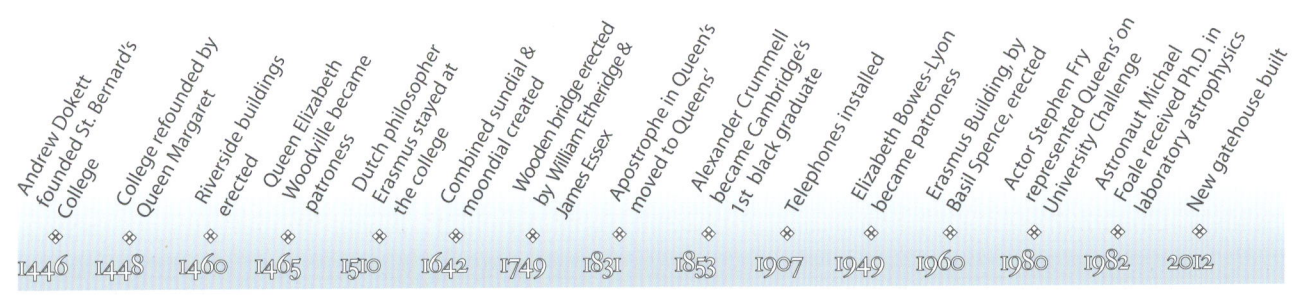

1446	Andrew Dokett founded St. Bernard's College
1448	College refounded by Queen Margaret
1460	Riverside buildings erected
1465	Queen Elizabeth Woodville became patroness
1510	Dutch philosopher Erasmus stayed at the college
1642	Combined sundial & moondial created
1749	Wooden bridge erected by William Etheridge & James Essex
1831	Apostrophe in Queen's moved to Queens'
1853	Alexander Crummell became Cambridge's 1st black graduate
1907	Telephones installed
1949	Elizabeth Bowes-Lyon became patroness
1960	Erasmus Building, by Basil Spence, erected
1980	Actor Stephen Fry represented Queens' on University Challenge
1982	Astronaut Michael Foale received Ph.D. in laboratory astrophysics
2012	New gatehouse built

18

ST CATHARINES

Robert Wodelark, the third Provost of King's College, founded St. Catharine's in 1473. During this time the college buildings faced Queens' College across *Milne Street*. This was a major thoroughfare when Cambridge was still a sea port, but today has become a shady cul-de-sac called Queens' Lane. St. Catharine's thrived with the backing of Henry VI, but struggled financially once he was overthrown. In 1626 however, the Master of Gonville & Caius, John Gosling, bequeathed the Bull Inn (to the dismay of his own college!) and more funds followed, donated by John Eachard. The college buildings turned around at the same time as its fortunes, to face King's Parade, and a new chapel was set on the former site of stables owned by carrier Thomas Hobson. In 1745, Mary Ramsden left her estate to St. Catharine's, enabling further new buildings. Notable members include John Addenbrooke, who founded Cambridge's famous hospital, and many recent TV and film celebrities.

1473	Robert Wodelark founded the college
1618	Dramatist John Shirley entered the college
1626	John Gosling bequeathed The Bull Inn to St. Catharine's
1675	Dr John Eachard funded new buildings
1697	John Addenbrooke entered the college
1704	New college chapel built
1730	Shakespeare expert Edward Capell entered the college
1745	Lady Ramsden's bequest funded further building, College re-oriented to face Trumpington Street
1847	Queen Victoria dined at St. Catharine's
1947	Library refurbished as the college's WW2 memorial
1966	Major rebuilding project begun, creating improved accommodation and facilities
1969	Journalist & TV presenter Jeremy Paxman entered the college
1991	Alumnus Sir Ian McKellen knighted for services to the Performing Arts
2013	McGrath Centre opened by Lord Sainsbury

JESUS

The Benedictine nunnery of St. Radegund received its charter in 1145 and thrived for many years. However, by 1496 it was in serious decline and John Alcock, Bishop of Ely, chose it to become *The College of the Blessed Virgin Mary, St. John the Evangelist and the Glorious Virgin St. Radegund*. Thankfully, the simpler name *Jesus College* prevailed. One of the most notable students was Thomas Cranmer, who won favour with Henry VIII by advising him on his first divorce and implementing his Reformation of the Church. Wayward poet Samuel Taylor Coleridge entered in 1791. He never took his degree, but loved "the friendly cloisters and happy grove of quiet, ever-honoured Jesus College". Today the college celebrates art. Its Second Court is adorned with curious natural forms of topiary yew trees, and the woodland grounds are interspersed with modern sculptures. These permanent installations are complemented by visiting works when the college hosts its biennial *Sculpture in the Close* exhibition.

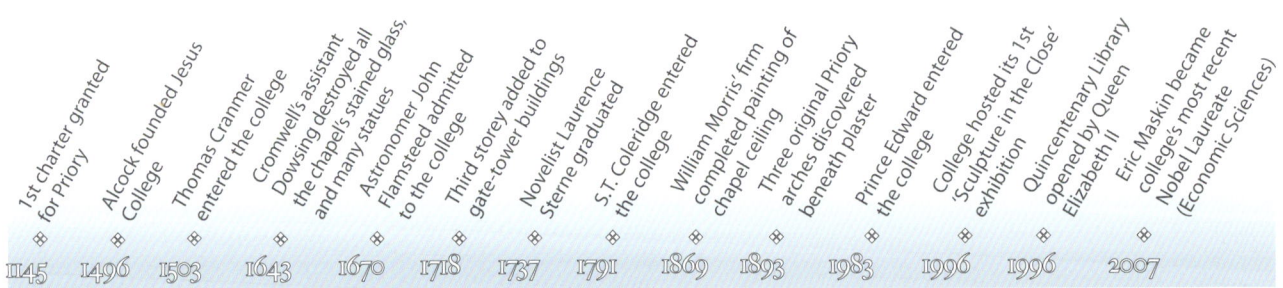

1145	1st charter granted for Priory
1496	Alcock founded Jesus College
1503	Thomas Cranmer entered the college
1643	Cromwell's assistant Dowsing destroyed all the chapel's stained glass, and many statues
1670	Astronomer John Flamsteed admitted to the college
1718	Third storey added to gate-tower buildings
1737	Novelist Laurence Sterne graduated
1791	S.T. Coleridge entered the college
1869	William Morris' firm completed painting of chapel ceiling
1893	Three original Priory arches discovered beneath plaster
1983	Prince Edward entered the college
1996	College hosted its 1st 'Sculpture in the Close' exhibition
1996	Quincentenary Library opened by Queen Elizabeth II
2007	Eric Maskin became college's most recent Nobel Laureate (Economic Sciences)

Founded in 1505 by Lady Margaret Beaufort, grandmother to Henry VIII. She was a highly intelligent, compassionate lady who cared greatly for the welfare of her students. The ornate heraldry displayed throughout the college illustrates her family name. In 1714 the college's original dilapidated stone and red brick walls were refaced with the smart stonework seen today. Christ's has some of Cambridge's finest architecture. It also has a swimming pool, fed by Hobson's Conduit. Poet John Milton studied here in 1625. In the beautiful, ancient gardens is a 400 year-old mulberry tree where, stories say, he liked to sit in contemplation. One of Christ's most notable members was Charles Darwin, who entered as a student in 1827, intending to become a clergyman. Ironically, his studies led him into conflict with the church over his theories published in *The Origin of Species* in 1859. Other members include philosopher William Paley, scientist Jagadish Chandra Bose, and satirist Sacha Baron-Cohen (Ali G & Borat!).

CHRIST'S

1439 — William Bingham founded God's House
1505 — God's House refounded as Christ's College by Lady Margaret
1509 — Earliest English wallpaper, discovered during 1900s, dated to this time
1609 — King James instigated planting of mulberry trees, to cultivate for silk trade
1625 — Poet John Milton entered college
1640 — Fellows' Building completed
1714 — Dilapidated red brick & clunch refaced along St. Andrew's Street
1770 — James Essex completed updating of First Court
1825 — Range of buildings completed on south side of second court
1827 — Charles Darwin entered the college
1897 — Old Library extended by G.F. Bodley
1966 — New Court Typewriter building by Sir Denys Lasdun
2007 — Sir Martin Evans became college's most recent Nobel Laureate (Medicine)
2009 — Darwin Bicentenary Garden & statue

21

ST JOHNS

Lady Margaret Beaufort's second college, St. John's, was founded in 1511. The beautiful crest above the Great Gate may also be seen at its sister foundation, Christ's College. The college replaced the Hospital of St. John the Evangelist, whose statue is also displayed on the Great Gate. He holds a chalice with a serpent, which represents the Devil, who had poisoned the contents but was driven out by the saint's prayers. The splendid chapel, at 50 metres, has the tallest tower in Cambridge. Across the road a statue of John Fisher adorns the Divinity School. This wise gentleman encouraged Lady Margaret to found the college, but was later beheaded for daring to disagree with Henry VIII's Church reformation. The college has nurtured many great careers including William Wilberforce, who fought to abolish slavery, poet William Wordsworth, and scientists Sir Edward Appleton, Sir John Cockroft & Abdus Salam. It has also educated 9 Nobel Prize winners, 6 prime ministers and 3 archbishops.

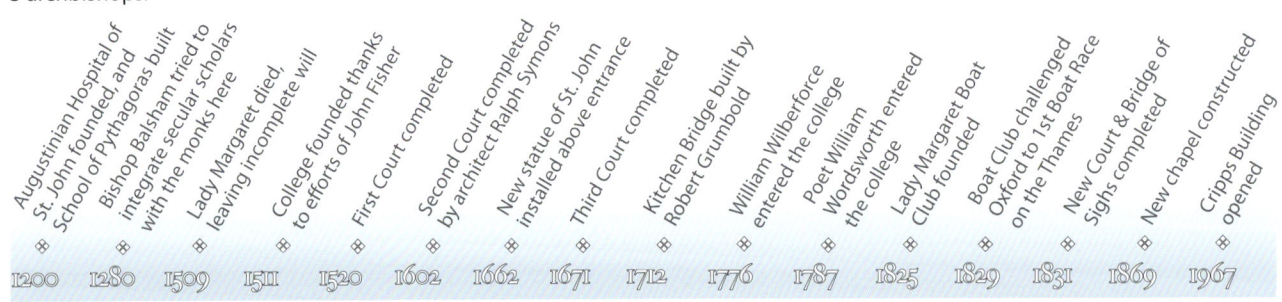

- 1200 — Augustinian Hospital of St. John founded
- 1280 — School of Pythagoras built
- 1509 — Bishop Balsham tried to integrate secular scholars with the monks here
- 1511 — Lady Margaret died, leaving incomplete will
- 1520 — College founded thanks to efforts of John Fisher
- 1602 — First Court completed
- 1662 — Second Court completed by architect Ralph Symons
- 1671 — New statue of St. John installed above entrance
- 1712 — Third Court completed
- 1776 — Kitchen Bridge built by Robert Grumbold
- 1787 — William Wilberforce entered the college
- 1825 — Poet William Wordsworth entered the college
- 1829 — Lady Margaret Boat Club founded
- 1831 — Boat Club challenged Oxford to 1st Boat Race on the Thames
- 1869 — New Court & Bridge of Sighs completed
- 1967 — New chapel constructed, Cripps Building opened

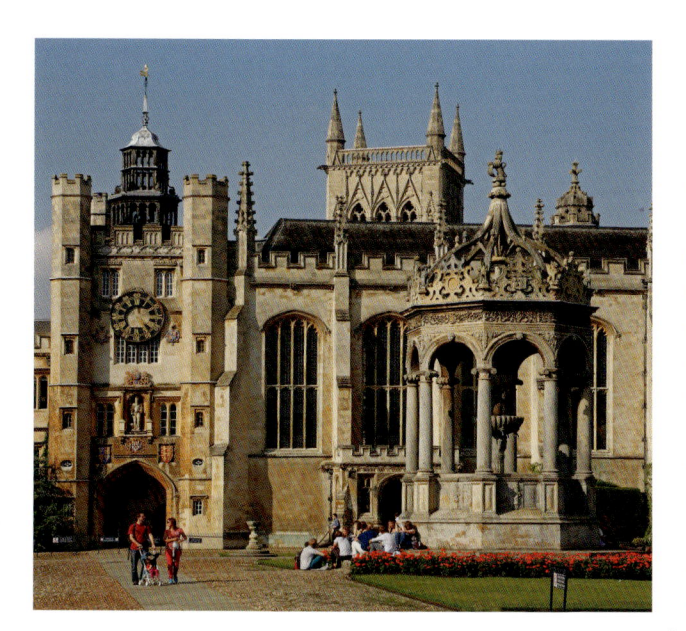

Everything about Trinity College is on a grand scale, just as one would expect from a college founded by King Henry VIII. When it was created in 1546, it absorbed two existing colleges along with a large area of the town. It has a mighty reputation, with 32 Nobel Prize winners, and alumni including Sir Isaac Newton, Alfred Tennyson, and HRH Prince Charles. A statue of Henry VIII stands above the Great Gate, his regal dignity only slightly diminished by the chair leg that replaced his sceptre in the 1800s as a student prank. The chapel was completed by Henry VIII's daughter Mary. It contains statues of Newton, Tennyson, and 'lion-like' Master, William Whewell. Trinity's magnificent library was designed, free of charge, by Sir Christopher Wren. It is said that poet Lord Byron enraged college officials by bathing in the fountain *(left)*. On the lawn outside the college is a small apple tree descended from that famous tree whose falling fruit inspired Sir Isaac Newton to the concept of gravity. His former rooms are to the right of the Great Gate.

TRINITY

1324	Michaelhouse founded by Hervey de Staunton
1337	King's Hall founded by Edward III
1535	Great Gate completed as part of King's Hall
1546	King Henry VIII founded Trinity College
1601	Original fountain installed
1612	Nevile's Court completed entirely at Nevile's own expense
1661	Newton entered the college
1695	Wren Library completed, designed free of charge by Sir Christopher Wren
1764	Trinity's bridge constructed
1805	Byron entered college, bringing a pet bear, as dogs were not allowed
1859	Whewell's Court completed
1904	Lord Rayleigh became Trinity's first Nobel Laureate (Physics)
1927	Lord Burghley completed circuit of Great Court within the clock's 'double' noon chimes
1967	Prince Charles entered the college to study archaeology, history & anthropology
2009	Venkatraman Ramakrishnan became Trinity's most recent Nobel Laureate (Chemistry)

EMMANUEL

In 1584 Sir Walter Mildmay raised the royal eyebrows of Queen Elizabeth I by founding a controversially Puritan college. Although he eloquently reassured the queen that he had "merely set an acorn", his new college chapel clearly demonstrated rejection of Catholic ideals, for it was oriented north-south, not the traditional east-west. The college burned with evangelical fervour, urged on by its charismatic Master, Laurence Chaderton, who could hold a congregation spellbound for over 2 hours. In the 1630s, John Harvard was among 35 Emmanuel scholars who sailed to America to spread the Word of God. Oliver Cromwell favoured its modest, Puritan ideals and chose 8 of its members to take over Royalist colleges in the 1640s. However, when the Royalists regained power, Emmanuel received a new chapel, designed by Sir Christopher Wren in 1677 (this time facing east-west!). The vast gardens contain many exceptional trees, and its pond dates from the 1500s when it was the fishpond for a Dominican Friary.

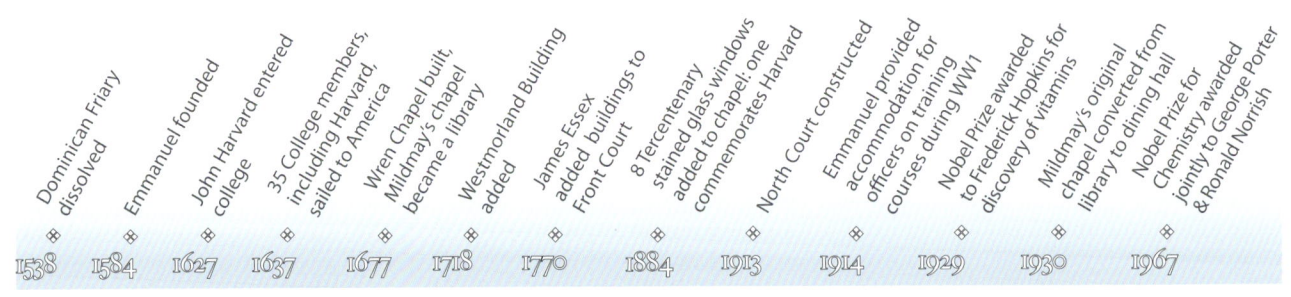

- 1538 — Dominican Friary dissolved
- 1584 — Emmanuel founded
- 1627 — John Harvard entered college
- 1637 — 35 College members, including Harvard, sailed to America
- 1677 — Wren Chapel built, Mildmay's chapel became a library
- 1718 — Westmorland Building added
- 1770 — James Essex added buildings to Front Court
- 1884 — 8 Tercentenary stained glass windows added to chapel: one commemorates Harvard
- 1913 — North Court constructed
- 1914 — Emmanuel provided accommodation for officers on training courses during WW1
- 1929 — Nobel Prize awarded to Frederick Hopkins for discovery of vitamins
- 1930 — Mildmay's original chapel converted from library to dining hall
- 1967 — Nobel Prize for Chemistry awarded jointly to George Porter & Ronald Norrish

24

SIDNEY SUSSEX

Sidney Sussex was founded in 1596, based on the site of a Franciscan friary which had been dissolved by Henry VIII. Much of the friary's stone was taken by Trinity College to build their chapel. Today, Sidney Sussex has its own beautiful chapel, and atmospheric cloisters where the paving is worn away by countless footsteps. The courtyard layout emulated Gonville & Caius - it was thought that this arrangement encouraged healthy air circulation and would reduce risk of plague. Sidney Sussex's most notable student was Oliver Cromwell, who studied here in 1616. Cromwell was beheaded posthumously by the re-established Royalists. Many years later, in 1960, his head was returned to the college and is now buried in the chapel. The cement facing and gables on the buildings today were added by architect Jeffery Wyatt, who was also commissioned by George IV for work on Windsor Castle. The vast lawns behind the college are remarkable in spring when they are carpeted with snowdrops, anemones and daffodils.

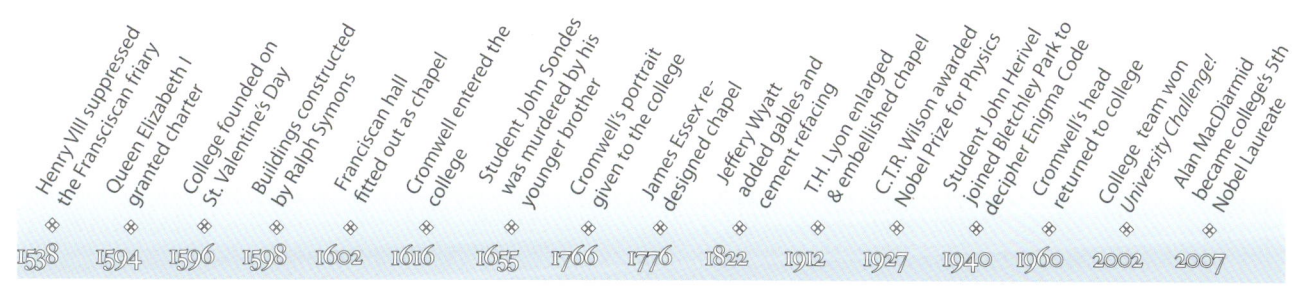

Timeline

- **1538** — Henry VIII suppressed the Franciscan friary
- **1594** — Queen Elizabeth I granted charter
- **1596** — College founded on St. Valentine's Day
- **1598** — Buildings constructed by Ralph Symons
- **1602** — Franciscan hall fitted out as chapel
- **1616** — Cromwell entered the college
- **1655** — Student John Sondes was murdered by his younger brother
- **1766** — Cromwell's portrait given to the college
- **1776** — James Essex re-designed chapel
- **1822** — Jeffery Wyatt added gables and cement refacing
- **1912** — T.H. Lyon enlarged & embellished chapel
- **1927** — C.T.R. Wilson awarded Nobel Prize for Physics
- **1940** — Student John Herivel joined Bletchley Park to decipher Enigma Code
- **1960** — Cromwell's head returned to college
- **2002** — College team won University Challenge!
- **2007** — Alan MacDiarmid became college's 5th Nobel Laureate

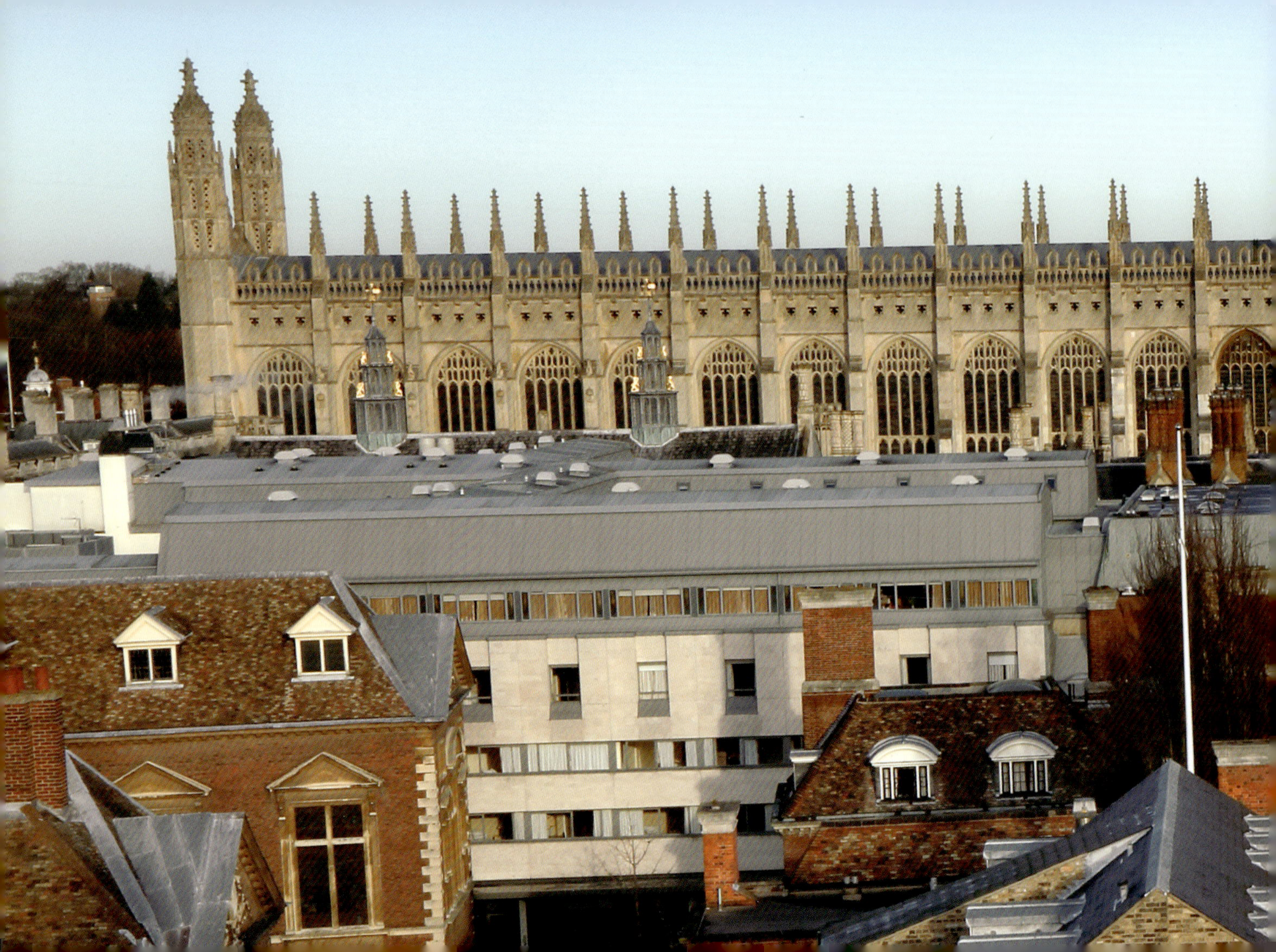

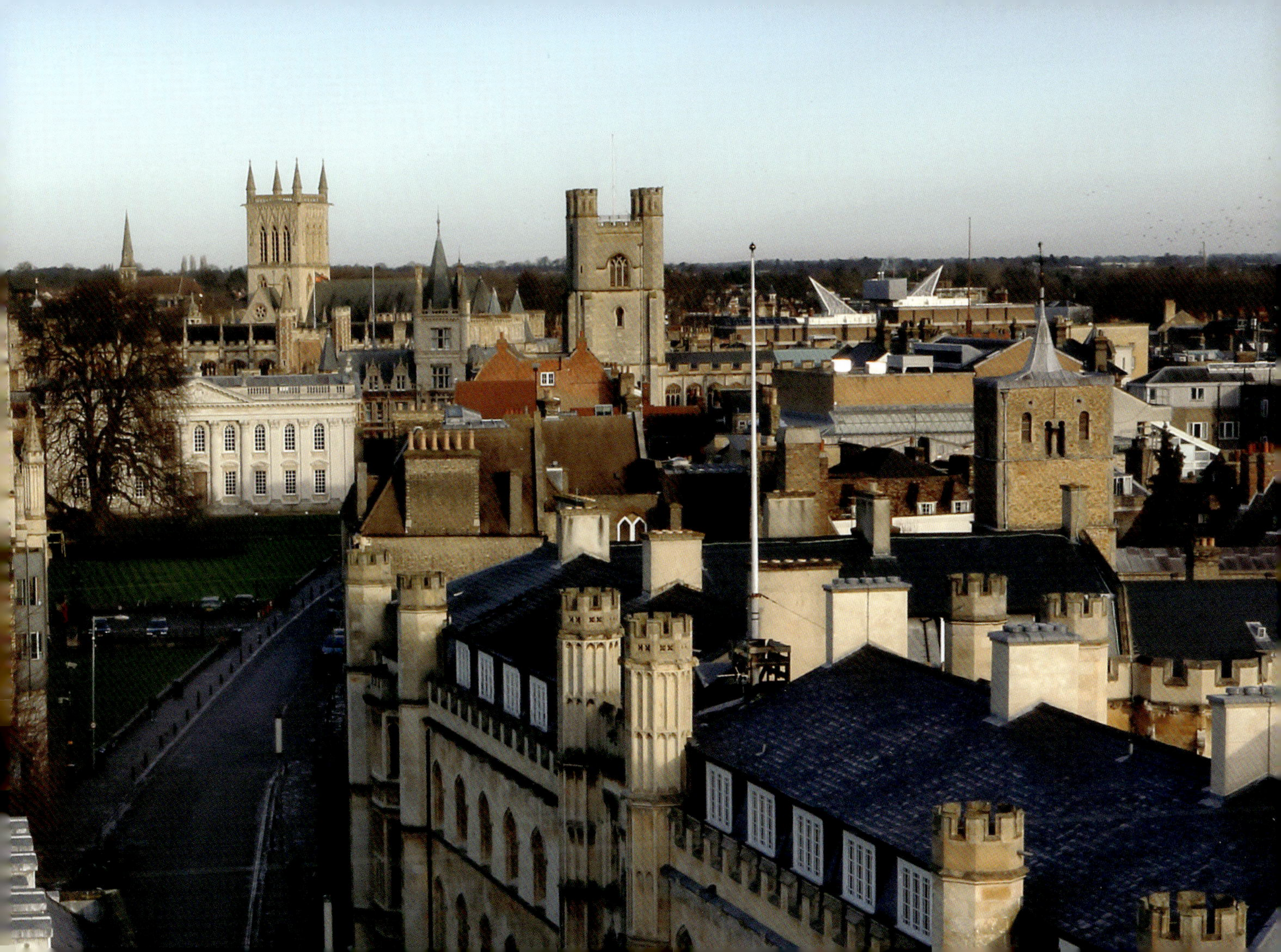

DOWNING

Downing's unique Classical buildings, begun in 1807, were designed by William Wilkins as King George III wished: in a style "definitely not Gothic". Sir George Downing had wanted the University to inherit his estate, but when he died in 1749, his estranged wife began a legal battle which would last for 80 years. The Downings, who owned the land occupied by 10, Downing Street in London, earned more money than popularity. Sir George himself was attacked with a hammer by an angry tenant because he "paid nobody, and was so ill a landlord and paymaster with so great an estate". In the late 1900s several benefactors financed a series of new developments. If the main quadrangle of Downing's buildings was completed, its area would trump Trinity College's Great Court. An urban myth tells that Trinity pays Downing an annual sum never to enclose this space, which would steal their claim to the largest court in Cambridge or Oxford. Downing's most familiar alumni are comedian John Cleese, BBC broadcaster Brian Redhead and artist Quentin Blake.

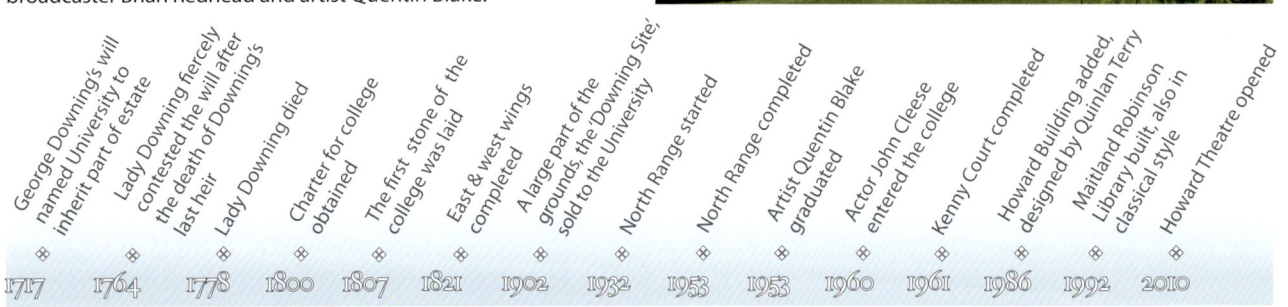

1717	George Downing's will named University to inherit part of estate
1764	Lady Downing fiercely contested the will after the death of Downing's last heir
1778	Lady Downing died
1800	Charter for college obtained
1807	The first stone of the college was laid
1821	East & west wings completed
1902	A large part of the grounds, the 'Downing Site', sold to the University
1932	North Range started
1953	North Range completed
1953	Artist Quentin Blake graduated
1960	Actor John Cleese entered the college
1961	Kenny Court completed
1986	Howard Building added, designed by Quinlan Terry
1992	Maitland Robinson Library built, also in classical style
2010	Howard Theatre opened

GIRTON

Girton, the first residential college for women, was initially based at Benslow House in Hitchin. It opened on 16th October, 1869 thanks to the efforts of Emily Davies, supported by Lady Stanley of Alderley and Madame Barbara Bodichon who donated generous funds. Emily Davies insisted that women should take the same Honours degree as Cambridge's male students, and Girton's first 5 students worked at this level, but University rules at that time denied them actual titles for their achievement. Benslow House soon proved too small, and with propriety in mind today's site, peripheral to Cambridge city centre, was selected. The new buildings opened in 1873, set amidst playing fields, woodland, and a beautiful orchard. Girton's outstanding library was built in 1884: its students could not access the main University libraries, and early donors of books include George Eliot and Tennyson. Girton specialises in the arts, and also has a rich musical tradition.

- **1869** – 1st five students began studies at Benslow House, Hitchin
- **1873** – New buildings designed by Alfred Waterhouse, opened in Cambridge
- **1876** – Lady Stanley funded the first laboratory
- **1881** – Anglo-Saxon cemetery & two Roman graves unearthed during building work
- **1891** – Lady Stanley died. College library renamed after her in 1895
- **1902** – Chapel Wing, Woodlands Wing & dining hall designed by Paul Waterhouse, son of the original architect
- **1948** – College awarded 1st woman's honorary degree to Queen Elizabeth the Queen Mother
- **1976** – Girton became one of the earliest co-educational colleges
- **2000** – Millennial People's Portraits exhibition mounted by Royal Society of Portrait Painters
- **2002** – New Swiss 4-manual mechanical action organ installed
- **2014** – Ash Court completed, winning 6 architectural & ecological awards

NEWNHAM

Women were first permitted to attend lectures at Cambridge in 1870, but had to commute to town daily. Millicent Garrett Fawcett, who became a celebrated campaigner for women's suffrage, realised that these ladies needed a place to stay in town. She urged philosopher Henry Sidgwick to risk his reputation by renting a Regent Street property for the young women, and in 1871 the first five students moved in, supervised by Anne Jemima Clough, who had run her own school in the Lake District. This little college had no official recognition, status, or money. However, demand soon increased. Newnham Hall, with its elegant *Queen Anne* style buildings set in spacious, informal grounds, opened its doors in 1875. The early senior Newnham members included some passionate horticulturists. They created the delightful gardens, which are often referred to as one of Cambridge's hidden secrets. Newnham today is run by women, for women, with alumnae including Sylvia Plath, Rosalind Franklin and Emma Thompson.

- **1871** — Newnham College first set up in Regent Street
- **1875** — Newnham Hall, designed by Basil Champneys, opened on present site
- **1881** — Women permitted to sit exams without making individual applications
- **1887** — Rebuffal of 1st attempt to secure titles for women's degrees as well as certificates
- **1890** — Millicent Fawcett's daughter Philippa shocked University by ranking 1st in the Mathematical Tripos
- **1897** — 2nd attempt to secure women's degree titles failed - male students rioted in the Market Square
- **1921** — Titles for degrees won, but full University inclusion denied - male students wrecked the college gates
- **1938** — Dorothy Garrod became 1st female Professor in Cambridge or Oxford
- **1948** — Women admitted to full University membership
- **1964** — Chemist Dorothy Hodgkin won the 1st women's Nobel Prize
- **2012** — Anna Watkins won an Olympic Gold Medal for rowing
- **2014** — Special Degree Ceremony held for women who graduated before 1948

Selwyn College was founded in 1882 for students "willing to live economically with a College wherein sober living and high culture of the mind may be combined with Christian training". The college was named after Bishop George Augustus Selwyn - the 1st Bishop of New Zealand. It remains true to its first egalitarian principles, as a broadly-based college with a higher-than-average percentage of students from state schools. Selwyn's development was hampered by financial limitations: not until 1929 were the last temporary buildings cleared away. For years it was misconceived by many as merely a training college for the clergy. Selwyn today is renowned for its music, but the sober repertoire of early days failed to please: the Master complained of audiences who "pelt the performers and interpolate choruses". Selwyn's alumni include John Gummer, Clive Anderson, and novelist Robert Harris. The physician and Olympic rowing gold medallist Ran Laurie also studied here, as did his son, Hugh Laurie.

SELWYN

- **1829** — George Augustus Selwyn rowed for Cambridge in the 1st Oxford-Cambridge Boat Race
- **1880** — Building began on 6 acres of land purchased from Corpus Christi
- **1882** — 1st Charter provided, & 28 students admitted
- **1914** — College let rooms to WW1 nurses; the lawns were used to grow hay and vegetables
- **1923** — Electricity installed
- **1929** — New Library built as a memorial to 70 students & 2 servants in WW1
- **1939** — College members manned the tower as a WW2 air raid warden's post
- **1948** — Selwyn's 1st May Ball
- **1958** — Selwyn achieved full college status within the University
- **1961** — The sunken courtyard filled in with spoil from building projects in Cambridge
- **1974** — Alumnus Clive Anderson was President of the Footlights dramatic society
- **1976** — Selwyn admitted women students
- **1980** — Alumnus & actor, Hugh Laurie competed in Oxford-Cambridge Boat Race
- **2008** — Selwyn ranked as highest achieving Cambridge undergraduate college

HUGHES HALL

Hughes Hall, the oldest of Cambridge's 6 post graduate colleges, began in 1885 when it was known as *The Cambridge Training College for Women*. This women-only status accounts for its location on the outskirts of town, where it overlooks the University's cricket ground, Fenners. By 1899 the college had 60 residential students, and had already trained over 500. Hughes Hall became a constituent society of the University in 1949, when it changed its name in honour of its first principal, Elizabeth Phillips Hughes. She advocated co-education from the outset, saying, "We shall never get first-rate training until men and women are trained together". In the 1960s it began to offer places to post-graduate students, and admitted men for the first time in 1970. Hughes Hall has strong links with the teaching profession: half its students take a Postgraduate Certificate in Education. Miss Hughes would be happy to see the international diversity and almost equal balance of men and women students today.

- **1885** — College began with 14 students, at Croft Cottage in Newnham
- **1895** — Today's site, designed by William Fawcett was opened
- **1902** — Elizabeth Hughes established overseas links in Japan
- **1949** — College renamed in celebration of women's admittance as full University members
- **1960** — Post-graduate students admitted for the first time
- **1970** — Hughes Hall began to accept male students
- **1985** — College became an Approved Foundation of the University
- **1995** — Chancellor's Court opened by HRH the Duke of Edinburgh
- **1997** — Centenary Building completed
- **2005** — Fenners Building built
- **2006** — Hughes Hall achieved full college status
- **2009** — Learning Resources Centre opened
- **2014** — College acquired former University gym to develop as a new facility

When Henry Fitzalan Howard, 15th Duke of Norfolk, funded this college in 1896, he ended 224 years of Catholic exile from Cambridge University. This had originated when the Test Act of 1672 banned Catholics from holding any public office. The college is named after St. Edmund of Abingdon (1175-1240), who was the first known Master of Arts at Oxford. St. Edmund's provided lodging for graduates from other Cambridge colleges, many of whom wished to enter the priesthood. Soon, however, most students came already ordained, to obtain a teaching qualification. The college's landmark tower was funded by a bequest from Dr Soichi Okinaga, and opened on 30th April, 1993 by the Right Honourable Betty Boothroyd. St. Edmund's remains oriented towards mature students, with 75% studying for higher degrees. Two thirds of its members are from overseas, comprising over 50 different nationalities. 2014 marked a new chapter, when the most recent Master, the Hon. Matthew Bullock, was elected.

1672	Test Act excluded Catholics from holding any public office
1871	Test Act repealed
1896	College founded: 4 students, led by Father Edmond Nolan, arrived in Cambridge on April 23rd
1896	On Nov. 2nd in the same year they moved into Ayerst Hostel - today's Norfolk Building
1916	College chapel blessed by Cardinal Francis Bourne
1923	Fr. Georges Lemaître researched his 'Big Bang' theory of the universe while living at the college
1939	Dining hall & extra student rooms completed
1965	1st four Fellows elected
1973	Catholic Church signed away the college buildings & land to the Master and Fellows
1975	College achieved Approved Foundation status
1993	Tower opened by the Right Honourable Betty Boothroyd
1996	St. Edmund's achieved full college status
2014	Hon. Matthew Bullock became Master

MURRAY EDWARDS

In 1954 Cambridge University had the lowest proportion of women students in the UK. The University responded by founding *New Hall*, the 3rd women's college. This began in premises where Darwin College currently stands, until its own first buildings were opened in 1965. Dame Rosemary Murray, the college's first President, held the position for 28 years. In 2008 *New Hall* was renamed *Murray Edwards College* in her honour, along with a former alumna, Ros Edwards, who donated £30 million. The world-class college art collection acquires work by female artists and promotes the success of women early in their career. The style of the college's neo-Byzantine dome *(right)* is continued in the elegant white arches of the vaulted library, which holds 65,000 works, including an important selection of feminist literature. The college celebrated its 60th anniversary in 2014. Its latest president is Dame Barbara Stocking, who was Chief Executive of Oxfam GB for 12 years.

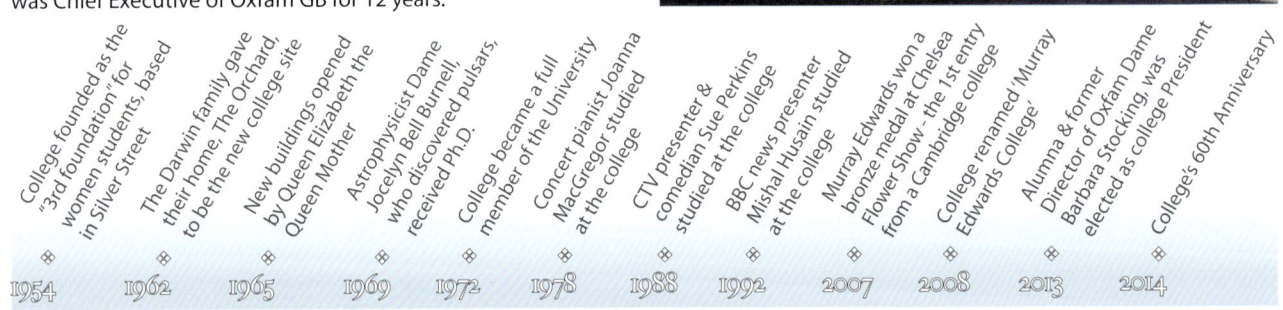

- 1954 — College founded as the "3rd foundation" for women students, based in Silver Street
- 1962 — The Darwin family gave their home, The Orchard, to be the new college site
- 1965 — New buildings opened by Queen Elizabeth the Queen Mother
- 1969 — Astrophysicist Dame Jocelyn Bell Burnell, who discovered pulsars, received Ph.D.
- 1972 — College became a full member of the University
- 1978 — Concert pianist Joanna MacGregor studied at the college
- 1988 — CTV presenter & comedian Sue Perkins studied at the college
- 1992 — BBC news presenter Mishal Husain studied at the college
- 2007 — Murray Edwards won a bronze medal at Chelsea Flower Show - the 1st entry from a Cambridge college
- 2008 — College renamed 'Murray Edwards College'
- 2013 — Alumna & former Director of Oxfam Dame Barbara Stocking, was elected as college President
- 2014 — College's 60th Anniversary

Sir Winston Churchill wished to create a college for the post-war modern age that could promote collaboration between industry and the universities. The building of his vision commenced on 17th October 1959. Churchill's Archives Centre holds documents of many significant political figures including Sir Winston and Baroness Thatcher. It is a major centre for recent history, providing insight into the minds of key figures who have shaped our world. Churchill specified that 70% of students should study mathematics or science: the college has never admitted a theology student. To support this, the college's first Master was nuclear physicist, Sir John Cockroft, followed by Sir William Hawthorne, a pioneer of the jet engine. Churchill has accrued 29 Nobel Prize winners to its name in just 60 years. In 1972 Churchill College became the first college to admit women students. The Møller Centre with its intriguing tower, is a major venue for conferences and management training, which opened in 1992.

CHURCHILL

1949	Churchill conceived the idea of a modern college while visiting Massachusetts Institute of Technology
1957	Nobel Chemist Alexander Todd recommended new scientific college at Cambridge
1958	National appeal to industry launched to raise £3.5 million for the project
1959	Site chosen - Sir Winston planted 2 trees during his sole visit.
1960	College received its Royal Charter and admitted first students
1965	Sir Winston Churchill died
1968	Final courtyard of original scheme opened
1972	Churchill College was the first all-male college to admit female students
1973	Churchill Archives Centre opened
1981	Churchill appointed a lay professional counsellor in place of a chaplain
1992	Møller Centre for Continuing Education opened
2002	BBC poll declared Sir Winston Churchill "the greatest Briton"
2014	College's 60th Anniversary

DARWIN

The 1960s saw a national shortage of postgraduate places. In 1964 three colleges: Gonville & Caius, Trinity and St. John's, collaborated to jointly found Darwin, Cambridge's first graduate-only college. The oldest part of the college, originally known as Newnham Grange, was built in 1793, and bought in 1885 by Sir George Darwin. It passed on to his son, Sir Charles, who died in 1962. When the University expressed interest in acquiring the property, Lady Darwin and her family were pleased to support the plans for a new college, and the name *Darwin College* was a natural choice for the new foundation. The college gradually expanded along Silver Street, buying up properties and adding new buildings. Darwin today provides a place of study and collaboration between Research Fellows, postdoctoral workers and students working towards Masters or Ph.D. degrees in a wide range of subjects. It is the University's largest postgraduate college, with around half of its 600 students today coming from over 50 countries.

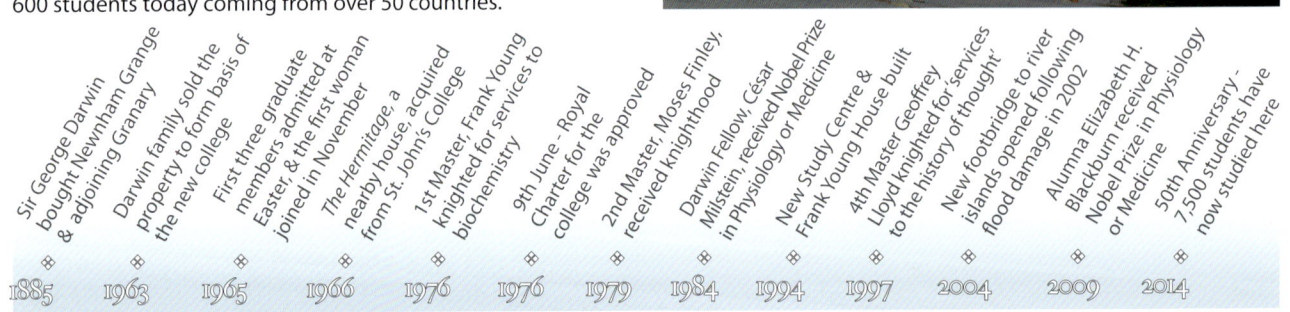

- **1885** – Sir George Darwin bought Newnham Grange & adjoining Granary
- **1963** – Darwin family sold the property to form basis of the new college
- **1965** – First three graduate members admitted at Easter, & the first woman joined in November
- **1966** – *The Hermitage*, a nearby house, acquired from St. John's College
- **1976** – 1st Master, Frank Young knighted for services to biochemistry
- **1976** – 9th June – Royal Charter for the college was approved
- **1979** – 2nd Master, Moses Finley, received knighthood
- **1984** – Darwin Fellow, César Milstein, received Nobel Prize in Physiology or Medicine
- **1994** – New Study Centre & Frank Young House built
- **1997** – 4th Master Geoffrey Lloyd knighted for 'services to the history of thought'
- **2004** – New footbridge to river islands opened following flood damage in 2002
- **2009** – Alumna Elizabeth H. Blackburn received Nobel Prize in Physiology or Medicine
- **2014** – 50th Anniversary – 7,500 students have now studied here

LUCY CAVENDISH

This is the most recent women's college in the United Kingdom. It began in 1965 as an academy for female graduates, thanks to three Newnham alumnae, Anna McClean Bidder, Kathleen Louise Wood-Legh, and Margaret Mary Braithwaite. They wished to resolve the isolation and frustrations brought by University rules that excluded women from Fellowships, even if they were actively engaged in teaching and research. In 1954 their Dining Group helped to persuade the University into founding New Hall, but women who held degrees were still excluded from fellowship at a college. The Dining Group applied for recognition as the Lucy Cavendish Collegiate Society, and in 1966; its first resident student, Peggy Seay, came from America to study for a Ph.D. in number theory. The college settled at Lady Margaret Road in 1970, with 10 graduate students, and in 1972 received its first 20 undergraduates. Today, Lucy Cavendish is the only women's college in Europe exclusively for students over 21.

- 1951 — Dining Group formed by 3 Newnham Alumnae
- 1954 — New Hall founded as a result of lobbying by their '3rd Foundation Association'
- 1964 — Dining Group obtained University recognition as the Lucy Cavendish Collegiate Society
- 1966 — Peggy Seay, the 1st student, came from U.S. to study Number Theory
- 1970 — College moved to new site in Lady Margaret Road with 10 graduate students
- 1972 — College numbers increased by additional 20 undergraduate students aged between 25 & 36
- 1989 — Her Majesty Queen Margrethe II of Denmark became an Honorary Fellow
- 1991 — Nearby Balliol Croft bought: converted into the President's Lodge in 2001
- 2003 — Dame Judi Dench was made an Honorary Fellow
- 2006 — Newscaster & journalist Anna Ford was made an Honorary Fellow
- 2014 — Political journalist & broadcaster Jackie Ashley appointed as the new college President
- 2015 — Lucy Cavendish College's 50th Anniversary

WOLFSON

Wolfson began in 1965 as *University College*, when the University perceived the needs of mature graduates coming from elsewhere to further their studies in Cambridge. It was initially based in Bredon House on the present site, when this was the only building, surrounded by orchard. The college gradually purchased nearby properties and erected new buildings, while creating surrounding gardens of exceptional interest. In 1973 the college name changed to *Wolfson* following a benefaction from the Wolfson Foundation, and the resulting buildings were opened by Queen Elizabeth II. The Lee Library was funded by a benefactor, Dr Lee Seng Tee, and opened in 1994. Its alumni include Zambia's President Rupiah Banda, Tharman Shanmugaratnam - Deputy Prime Minister of Singapore, Malaysian skyscraper architect Ken Yeang and Procol Harem organist, Matthew Fisher. Wolfson Fine Arts holds a series of temporary exhibitions which are open to the public.

1965	'University College' opened at Bredon House
1967	Alumnus Matthew Fisher played Hammond organ on Procol Harum's 'A Whiter Shade of Pale'
1970	Development of East and West Court accommodation began
1973	College renamed following a major benefaction from the Wolfson Foundation
1977	New buildings opened by Queen Elizabeth II
1992	Alumna Zhang Xin, the world's 7th richest self-made woman received her Master's Degree at Wolfson
1994	Lee Seng Tee Library opened
2004	Chancellor's Centre was completed
2008	Alumnus Rupiah Banda became President of Zambia
2011	Gardens opened under National Gardens Scheme
2011	Alumnus Ken Yeang designed Great Ormond Street Children's Hospital Extension
2011	Honorary Fellow Tharman Shanmugaratnam became Deputy Prime Minister of Singapore
2015	Wolfson's 50th Anniversary

CLARE HALL

Clare Hall was part of the 1960s' initiative to provide more fellowship posts in the University, as both research and diversity of graduate teaching were developing rapidly. Clare College wanted to improve post-graduate provision, but what form should it take? Should a separate centre be provided, or more senior academics brought into Clare's College fellowship? The dilemma was resolved by Richard Eden's suggestion:

> "the aim should be to establish a Society of Fellows primarily engaged in advanced study, to bring together an international community of scholars and Cambridge University lecturers and professors".

Clare Hall opened in 1966, designed to support not only scholars, but also their families. Clare College provided its first land and buildings, and remained its trustee until 1984. The college hosts a prestigious annual series of lectures known as the Tanner Symposium, and its alumni include several Nobel Prize winners.

- 1965 — Brian Pippard elected as 1st college President
- 1966 — Clare Hall created as a new college
- 1967 — Neighbouring house, Elmside, converted into rooms for graduate research students
- 1969 — College buildings formally opened by Sir Eric Ashby
- 1973 — Visiting Fellow Ivor Gaever received Nobel Prize for Physics
- 1978 — A nearby house was purchased, now known as Leslie Barnett House
- 1987 — Joseph Brodsky, poet in residence in 1977, awarded Nobel Prize for Literature
- 1996 — Former family home of Lord Rothschild bought and developed as Clare Hall West Court
- 2000 — Clare Hall hosted the millennial Tanner Symposium
- 2000 — Former Visiting Fellow, Kim Dae-Jung, President of South Korea, received the Nobel Peace Prize
- 2008 — Work on plans for a new International Study & Research Centre began
- 2008 — Sir Martin Harris became Clare Hall's 7th President

FITZWILLIAM

For nearly a century, 'Fitzwilliam House' stood opposite the museum with which it shares its name, providing access to a Cambridge education for less affluent students. In 1963 it moved to Huntingdon Road, and became *Fitzwilliam College* in 1966, when the college's new buildings, by Sir Denys Lasdun, were finished. These form a striking contrast to the original house, *The Grove,* which once belonged to the Darwin family. Building has continued in adventurous and award-winning architectural style, culminating with the Olisa Library, which opened in 2010. The bold contours of Fitzwilliam's architecture are softened by the skillfully planted gardens. The college became co-educational in 1978, and today is home to 450 undergraduates, 300 graduates and 90 fellows. True to its origins, it combines Cambridge college traditions with an unpretentious, inclusive atmosphere where ability, not background, matters most.

1869	Fitzwilliam House opened opposite Fitzwilliam Museum
1932	Alumnus Sir Charles Scott Sherrington won Nobel Prize for work on function of the neuron
1937	Alumnus Albert Szent-Györgi won Nobel Prize for discovery of Vitamin C
1960	Start of new Hall & Central Building, Sir Denys Lasdun's 1st University project
1963	College moved to present site on Huntingdon Road
1966	College received Royal Charter & became Fitzwilliam College
1978	College admitted female students
1984	Alumnus César Milstein won Nobel Prize for developing monoclonal antibodies
1985	New Court opened, won David Urwin Award for Best New Building in 1989
1991	Chapel completed - won David Urwin Award for Best New Building in 1993
1994	Wilson Court added, designed by van Heyingen & Hayward Architects
1994	Gatehouse Court completed, later awarded BDA Building of the Year
2010	Olisa Library opened, designed by Edward Cullinan Architects
2013	Mathematician Arran Fernandez became youngest ever Senior Wrangler at age 18

HOMERTON

Homerton began in London as a society to train young men as ministers. It was founded by the Congregational Church in 1730, and convened every week at an inn, becoming known as the *King's Head Society*. In 1768 it bought premises of its own in Homerton High Street, and for a while it was affiliated to New College in London. When the Congregational Board of Education refounded it in 1850, Homerton became a specialist teacher training college for men and women. In 1894 it moved from the industrialised East End to Cambridge. A mixed college was unacceptable to the University, so the college changed to accept women only, but it reverted to being co-educational in 1976. It began to offer the complete academic range of courses in 2001 and nine years later became a full member of the University. Teaching degrees now form only a minor percentage of the subject range. Homerton today is Cambridge's largest college: Trinity is the only other college with more than 1000 students.

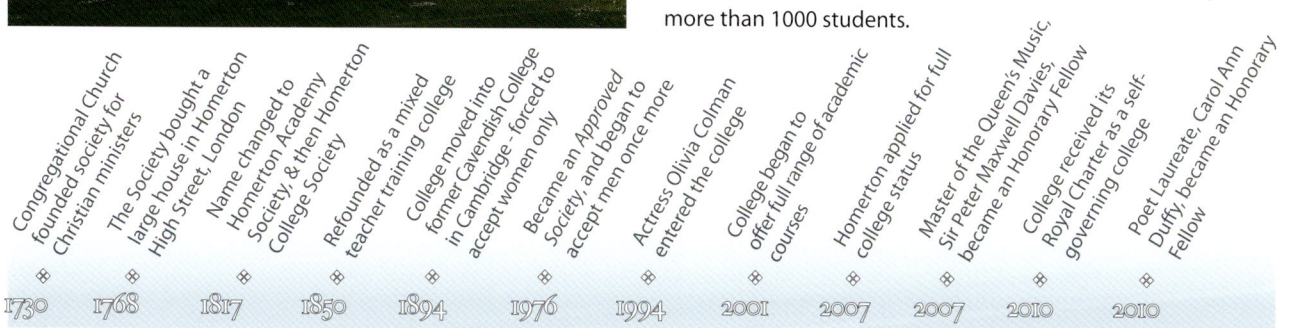

1730	Congregational Church founded society for Christian ministers
1768	The Society bought a large house in Homerton High Street, London
1817	Name changed to Homerton Academy Society, & then Homerton College Society
1850	Refounded as a mixed teacher training college
1894	College moved into former Cavendish College in Cambridge - forced to accept women only
1976	Became an Approved Society, and began to accept men once more
1994	Actress Olivia Colman entered the college
2001	College began to offer full range of academic courses
2007	Homerton applied for full college status
2007	Master of the Queen's Music, Sir Peter Maxwell Davies, became an Honorary Fellow
2010	College received its Royal Charter as a self-governing college
2010	Poet Laureate, Carol Ann Duffy, became an Honorary Fellow

ROBINSON

Sir David Robinson was a remarkable philanthropist and entrepreneur, whose fortune came chiefly from his television and rentals business, and later, horse racing. Robinson College, the newest in the University, was founded in 1979 thanks to his donation of £18 million. Its modern architecture features elements of a castle theme, evoked in the drawbridge-like path up to the entrance gate and tower. The buildings are faced with over one million handmade bricks. This is the only undergraduate college founded as co-educational from the outset. The multi-denominational chapel has a beautiful *Light of the World* stained glass window. This was designed by John Piper, as Sir David requested, to inspire people of all religious persuasions or none. The college's grounds are a surprising natural haven, comprising 10 original Edwardian gardens. Its spring flowers beside the lake and stream can rival any in the University, and the college is part of the National Gardens Scheme.

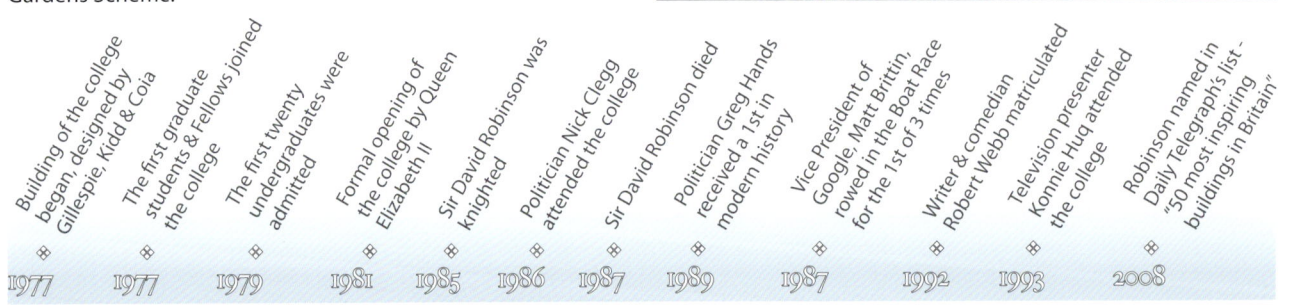

1977	Building of the college began, designed by Gillespie, Kidd & Coia
1977	The first graduate students & Fellows joined the college
1979	The first twenty undergraduates were admitted
1981	Formal opening of the college by Queen Elizabeth II
1985	Sir David Robinson was knighted
1986	Politician Nick Clegg attended the college
1987	Sir David Robinson died
1989	Politician Greg Hands received a 1st in modern history
1987	Vice President of Google, Matt Brittin, rowed in the Boat Race for the 1st of 3 times
1992	Writer & comedian Robert Webb matriculated
1993	Television presenter Konnie Huq attended the college
2008	Robinson named in Daily Telegraph's list - "50 most inspiring buildings in Britain"

FITZWILLIAM MUSEUM

Richard, seventh Viscount Fitzwilliam, was a keen art collector. In 1816 he bequeathed his library, collection of paintings, and £100,000 to the University to build a place worthy of housing them. Today the Fitzwilliam Museum is home to half a million treasures of national and international significance including Egyptian, Roman and Greek collections. There are also exhibits of coins, ceramics, and textiles, not to mention an impressive selection of armour and weapons, guaranteed to delight any young would-be warrior. The extensive collection of ancient and modern manuscripts includes John Keats' *Ode to a Nightingale*, an important series of Handel manuscripts, and autographed compositions by Purcell, Bach and Mozart. The range of art encompasses works from Rembrandt and Rubens to Picasso and Barbara Hepworth. The collection is constantly evolving, and regularly hosts additional visiting collections. The Fitzwilliam is described today as "One of the greatest art collections of the nation and a monument of the first importance".

1816	Viscount Fitzwilliam's bequest to the University - art collection housed at the Perse School
1822	1st Egyptian artefacts donated to the Museum
1837	Foundation stone of Museum was laid
1842	Art collection moved to the Old Schools; - the University Library at that time
1845	Museum architect George Basevi died in a fall at Ely Cathedral
1848	Basevi's 'Founder's Building' completed by C.R. Cockerell
1861	John Ruskin donated 25 Turner watercolour drawings; Sir Sydney Cockerell added 8 more
1875	Entrance Hall built, designed by Edward Middleton Barry
1912	Charles Brinsley Marlay bequeathed 84 paintings & £80,000
1931	2-storey extension added, partly funded by a donation from the Courtauld family
2006	Three large oriental vases were shattered when a visitor tripped and fell
2012	18 Chinese works of art stolen - burglars sentenced to combined 18 years jail
2014	Museum experts confirmed the Rothschild bronze figures are by Michelangelo

BOTANIC GARDEN

Cambridge Botanic Garden, founded in 1762 "for the benefit of mankind", first occupied a 5-acre site donated by Trinity's Reverend R. Walker. Set between Downing Street and Free School Lane, the garden there emulated the Physic Garden at Chelsea. Charles Darwin's teacher, Steven Henslow, believed that the study of plants had more to offer than just their medicinal properties and proposed the move to a larger site. Land was acquired from Trinity Hall in 1831 and the new 40-acre garden opened 15 years later, on November 2nd 1846. The first curator, Andrew Murray, devised the basic layout with its winding path around the circumference, the lake, magnificent arboretum and systematic beds. The gates from the original garden were relocated to the Trumpington Road side by Hobson's Conduit, from which the garden takes its water supply. Today's entrance is via award-winning new gates on the corner of Brookside and Trumpington Road. The Garden is a research centre of international significance, containing around 8,000 plant species.

- 1762 — Original Botanic Garden founded closer to the town centre
- 1796 — Curator James Donn published 1st edition of Hortus Cantabrigiensis - cataloguing the Garden plants
- 1825 — John Henslow accepted the Chair of Botany - a weak subject in the University at this time
- 1831 — Land acquired from Trinity Hall to establish the new Garden
- 1846 — The new Garden officially opened but only half the site was developed initially
- 1860 — Construction of Glasshouses began, plus the 1st English example of a Rock Garden
- 1904 — The Garden began supplying data to the Meteorological Office at Bracknell
- 1909 — Original gate moved to the Trumpington Road edge of the Garden
- 1921 — H. Gilbert-Carter appointed as the Garden's first scientific Director
- 1924 — Reginald Cory, of Trinity College, gave money to build Cory Lodge
- 1934 — Reginald Cory died; his legacy allowed the Garden to consider developing its unused 20

The Glasshouse Range displays 2,000 specimens in carefully replicated jungle, desert and alpine environments. With a focus on aspects of climate change, ecology and sustainable horticulture, minimal irrigation and chemical intervention is used. A weather station supplying data to the Meteorological Office at Bracknell is also located here. The Garden's newest development, the Sainsbury Laboratory, houses the University Herbarium (*left*): a collection of over 1,000,000 pressed plant specimens, including some collected by Charles Darwin. The Garden's main purpose may be scientific study, but its beauty enchants visitors of all ages. Children love to run in the grass maze and explore the rockery. The fountain, designed by silversmith David Mellor, fascinates everybody. Even in the depths of winter, colour, scent and a wonderful tapestry of natural forms delight the senses, and wildlife is abundant. Whether you choose to wander through the grounds, or find a shady sanctuary to absorb the peace, the Botanic Garden is a perennial joy.

1943	Cory's legacy turned out to be much larger than first believed: half a million pounds!
1951	Creation of new Garden area begun by Superintendent, Bob Younger, and John Gilmour
1958	Limestone Rock Garden created beside the lake
1981	The Garden was designated holder of 9 National Plant Collections by Plant Heritage
2008	Award-winning new gates opened by HRH the Duke of Edinburgh
2009	New 'Mountains Display' opened in the Glasshouse Range
2011	Sainsbury Laboratory, funded by Lord Sainsbury, was opened by Queen Elizabeth II
2012	Sainsbury Laboratory building won RIBA Stirling Prize
2013	New perennial wild flower meadow created
2015	Innovative P2P (Plant to Power) self-powering bus-shelter displayed at the Garden

BOTANIC GARDEN

45

INDEX

Actors 8,10,18,19,21,28,30, 31,37,41,42
Addenbrookes Hospital: 4,19
Architects 7,8,9,10,15,18, 21,23,24,25,29,38,40,43
Art 12,13,20,28,29,34,37,43
Authors 14,19,31,34,39

Bishops 6,8,12,13,20,22,31
Black Death 4,6,12,13
Boat Race 7,22,31,42
Botanic Garden 7,44-45
Broadcasting 5,9,15,28,31, 34,37,42

Catholics 8,11,24,33
Christ's College 6,21
Churches 4,12
Churchill College 7,35
Civil War 4,5,8,13,15
Clare College 4,6,9
Clare Hall 7,39
Corpus Christi 6,7,13,31
Cromwell,Oliver 4,5,10,20,24

Darwin 7,34,36,40,45
Downing College 7,28

Emmanuel College 6,24

Fitzwilliam College 7,40
Fitzwilliam Museum 7,12,43

Gardens 8,9,12,20,21,24, 25,29,30,34,38,40,42
Girton College 7,29
Gonville & Caius 6,11,19,25

Henry VIII 4,14,15,20,21, 22,23,25
Hobson's Conduit 4,8,19,21
Homerton College 7,41
Hughes Hall 7,32

Jesus College 4,20

King's College 6,15,16-17, 19,46

Lucy Cavendish 7,37

Magdalene College 6,7,14
Monasteries 6,14,20,22, 24,25
Murray Edwards 7,34
Music 5,9,12,14,15,31, 34,38,41,43,

Newnham College 7,30
Nobel Prize 8,11,20,21, 22,23,24,25,30,35,36,39,40

Oxford 6,7,8,11,12,28, 30,31,33

Pembroke College 6,10
Peterhouse 6,8
Poets 10,15,19,20,21, 22,23,30,39,41,43

Postgraduates 32,33,36, 37,38
Prime Ministers 10,15,22, 35,38,39,42

Queens' College 4,6,18,19

River Cam 4,12,18,36
Robinson College 7,42
Rowing 7,22,31
Royalty 5,10,15,18,19,20, 21,22,23,24,25,28,29,32, 34,37,38,42,45

Scientists 8,11,12,21,22, 23,24,30,33,34,35,39,40,45
Selwyn College 7,31
Sidney Sussex 6,7,25
St. Bene't's Church 4
St. Catharine's 6,19
St. Edmund's College 7,33
St. John's College 6,22,36

Trinity College 6,14,23,25, 28,36,41
Trinity Hall 6,9,12,44

University 4,5,6,7,28, 29,38

Wolfson College 7,38
Women 6,7,9,15,29, 30,32,34,35,37,41
WW1 9,10,24,31
WW2 15,19,25,31

Corpus Christi Clock, 2008

48